9.

Images
and the Imageless

Images and the Imageless

A Study in Religious Consciousness and Film

Thomas M. Martin

Lewisburg
Bucknell University Press
London and Toronto: Associated University Presses

Associated University Presses, Inc.
4 Cornwall Drive
East Brunswick, New Jersey 08816

Associated University Presses
69 Fleet Street
London EC4Y 1EU, England

Associated University Presses
Toronto M5E 1A7, Canada

Library of Congress Cataloging in Publication Data

Martin, Thomas M   1940–
   Images and the imageless.

   Bibliography: p.
   Includes index.
   1. Religion and motion pictures. I. Title.
PN1995.5.M37   791.43'09'09382   79-57611
ISBN 0-8387-5005-2

Printed in the United States of America

For Mary Ann

Contents

Preface
Acknowledgments
1 Introduction   1
2 Images, the Medium, and   37
  Religious Consciousness
3 Imaginative Constructs and   59
  Religious Consciousness
4 Religious Reflection, Films,   113
  and Stories
5 Film Criticism as Establishing Sequence   129
  for Religious Studies
6 Religion and the Use of Films   155
  Appendix: Some Unique Questions   165
  About Television
  Bibliography   171
  Index   175

Preface

Religious studies have maintained a tradition of dialogue with poetry, fiction, and the dramatic arts. Those engaged in probing religious consciousness have long recognized that many of the concerns expressed in poetry, for example, were similar to the struggles they were encountering in their own discipline. As a result, the mid-twentieth century has seen sophisticated methodologies developed in what is commonly called religion and literature studies. Rather than give a detailed description of the different approaches in this field, I refer the reader to Giles Gunn's excellent introduction to the volume *Religion and Literature* (New York: Harper and Row, 1971). There the editor provides a good summary of how, depending on their theory of literature, the writers in this discipline have nuanced their approaches.

The other forms of art also overlap with the religious concerns and articulations of a people. Painting, sculpture, and music have always had an overt role in the religious life of most Western religions. Unfortunately, the methodologies for relating these different forms to religious expression are not developed so decisively. The end result has often been a rather haphazard discussion of this or that aspect of art or religion without offering a firm foundation to many of the implied presuppositions. Works such as Gerardus van der Leeuw's *Sacred and Profane Beauty* (New York: Holt, Rinehart and Winston, Inc., 1963) and the more recent works by F. David

Martin and John W. Dixon are examples of the valuable work that is developing.

Given these efforts of religious studies to relate to the art forms of the culture, one would expect a similar developing methodology for confronting film since its impact on present society's values and identity is indisputable. Unfortunately, however, the discipline is young and the methodologies are at best in their formative stages. There have been excellent initial works such as Paul Schrader's *Transcendental Style in Film* (Berkeley: University of California Press, 1972), in which after briefly struggling with some initial questions of methodology, the author moves into the study of three given directors. There have been collections of essays such as John C. Cooper's and Carl Skrade's *Celluloid and Symbols* (Philadelphia: Fortress Press, 1970) and James M. Wall's *Church and Cinema* (Grand Rapids: William B. Eerdman's Publishing Company, 1971). Although one can find many helpful pieces in these books, the burden of relating film and religious studies is carried by a comment here and there about isolated themes without any overall methodology.

In contrast, Neil P. Hurley's *Theology Through Film* (New York: Harper and Row, 1970) offers a disciplined and valuable approach to the themes of modern films, but does not give enough systematic attention to the film as a medium. As the title itself suggests, films are often used to present issues of religious concern and are not studied on their own merits. Other books such as Arthur Gibson's *The Silence of God* (New York: Harper and Row, 1969) and Ernest Ferlita's and John May's *Film Odyssey: The Art of Film as Search for Meaning* (New York: Paulist Press, 1976), as well as their more recent *The Parables of Lina Wertmuller* (New York: Paulist Press, 1977), take films seriously and certainly probe the religious concern more than the books in the late 1950s and early 1960s that treated the morals of movies. The more recent titles, then, do attempt to deal in some general terms with film as a medium. But the focus is not broad enough.

To some extent, therefore, this small volume attempts to cover new ground. It attempts to relate the film medium to religious studies by means of the spatial interpretation and orientation (the image, the sense of direction) that is common to both forms of reflection. On the one hand, this work appreciates the film as a medium of images that persistently affects the individual and collective spatial origins of thought found in our culture and therefore must be taken into account by any exercise in religious consciousness. It respects film as having its own dynamics that must be treated on their own terms. But precisely because it has its own dynamics and claims a large portion of many people's time, it must have an impact on all forms of human reflection.

On the other hand, because the religious quest is a probing of human identity at such a basic level, it will permeate all of the articulations of the human culture including film. Perhaps the influence will not be seen in any explicit terms. But certainly the basic movements of a people's identity will be present in their art forms, particularly a popular art form such as film.

Acknowledgments

The University of Dayton provided assistance for this study through a summer fellowship and a sabbatical. I am also indebted to Julie Suba and Michael Barnes for their specific help and encouragement with the project and to William P. Frost and Matthew Kohmescher, S.M., for their general encouragement. A number of colleagues such as Xavier Monasterio and John D. Ryan have offered helpful suggestions, and Betsy Hetrick is to be thanked for her work with the final manuscript. I would also like to thank my wife, Mary Ann; my parents, George and Agnes; and other members of my family, Brian, Shawn, Ernest, and Martha, for their help and encouragement.

I would also like to acknowledge *St. Luke's Journal of Theology* for permission to use some material that originally appeared in their publication.

1
Introduction

THOMAS MERTON always wondered at any goodness and value nurtured in a middle-class culture. When faced with his admiration for Thérèse of Lisieux, for example, he was "astonished" to find a saint "in the midst of all the stuffy, overplush, overdecorated, comfortable ugliness and mediocrity of the bourgeoise."[1] Given the sensitivities that he nurtured in his own life and the nuanced vision that he inherited from the paintings and person of his father, he simply had an impatience with the careless dynamics that characterized the insulated lives of most middle-class existences.

The struggle was most intense and the appreciation far more tempered when he came to terms with his grandparents, Pop and Bonnemaman. They did much for the young Merton—their generosity was undeniable. But he was continually repelled by the way they consumed rather than encountered. In Merton's eyes they sought a continual stimulation from the world rather than a dialogue. As a result their lives were summed up in gross and simplistic images that did violence to Merton's more nuanced grasp of life. For him such violations of the poetic vision could not be ignored. There was a constant struggle between Merton's appreciation of their basic goodness and his disgust with their lack of vision.

Nowhere is the negative tension more apparent than in his comments about his grandparents' love affair with movies. Instead of having a vision of depth in their lives, he saw these two older people whom he loved being sucked into the trivial rituals and symbols of the dominant popular art form, the movies.

> But to Pop and Bonnemaman, Doug and Mary seemed to sum up every possible human ideal: in them was all perfection of beauty and wit, majesty, grace and decorum, bravery and love, gaiety and tenderness, all virtues and every admirable moral sentiment, truth, justice, honor, piety, loyalty, zeal, trust, citizenship, valor and above all, marital fidelity.[2]

The judgment of this passage is harsh. And Merton is no easier on himself when, as a Trappist monk, he reflects on his college days and what he judged to be a sinful waste of his own time during a summer of discontent when he "would wander off to some appalling movie."[3] He speaks of his addiction to "those yellow flickering lights" and "the suffering of having to sit and look at such collossal stupidities" to the point where he "sometimes actually felt physically sick."[4]

His comments on the medium were not all negative. He speaks of his appreciation for Russian movies, René Clair, and the Marx brothers[5] and acknowledges "a secret loyalty to the memory of my great heroes: Chaplin, W. C. Fields, Harpo Marx, and many others."[6]

Merton, of course, was not a film critic. He did not go into any extensive theories of how films shape and mold audiences. In all probability he did not see a single film in the last twenty years of his life. But he was a keen observer of how one's values and images are formed by a web of seemingly insignificant events. He did realize that movies were not simple diversions from life or a form of innocent entertainment. Nothing can be perfunctorily dismissed by one who realizes the profound impact of any extended experience.

This is the contention that this volume wishes to offer: the persistent experience of electronically transmitted stories has a profound impact on the basic notion of oneself as it relates to one's religious sense of reality. As one views films and television with any regularity, heroes are bound to develop; and they will embody "all virtues and every admirable moral sentiment" as they did for Merton's grandparents. Even if one is simply "killing time" before the television in somewhat the same disgusted manner that Merton frequented the movie theaters, one is being presented with life stories that demand selection. The demand for choice is persistent; the effects are subtle yet profound.

But heroes are strange creatures. They do not confront one as a simple idea. They address themselves to many different levels of human consciousness and are accepted or rejected to the extent that they adequately meet the demands of these human dimensions. In some attempt, therefore, to acknowledge this complexity, this study develops four major facets. First, attention will be given to film as a medium and its ability to shape governing images. Secondly, it will expand the concept of image into its explicitly interpretive forms under the term "imaginative construct." Thirdly, it will speak of stories as developments that emerge from the basic imaginative constructs. And finally, it will examine the major concerns of the film critics to surface the implications of their studies for religious concerns. These major chapters will be followed by an appendix that will treat the uniqueness of television as a medium.[7]

Images

The study, therefore, emphasizes four pivotal terms—image, imaginative construct, story, and religious. The first consideration should be given to what appears to be

the most basic term—image. The term has a long, complicated history in Western thought; but in the perspective of
the study, several points must be clearly established. First, an
image suggests some type of picture—a spatial arrangement.
Secondly, as is any arrangement, an image is interpretive.
And finally, this interpretation is basic to human understanding and, given the unity of human reflection, will have an impact on all verbal articulation including religious reflection.
This dependency and unity of thought holds true whether or
not one is conscious of one's images. As Thomas Gornall notes
in an essay on the role of imagination in theology, many are
not sensitive to the phantasms out of which their abstract
thinking develops, but they are nevertheless basic.[8]

Of the three points emphasized, most would have little difficulty accepting the existence of images in their lives. Most
are aware of them playing some role in daily thought. With a
minimum of prompting, an individual can realize that images
are the dominant medium in sleep dreams and daydreams. In
themselves these activities occupy a large portion of one's
reflection. With a bit more prompting one can further realize
to what extent even the more disciplined reflection that uses
words as its principal medium also depends on images as it
freely employs metaphors. To see images as an intricate part
of one's thought is not difficult, therefore; but to see images as
interpretive and, more important, as having an impact on all
human interpretation may not be accepted as readily. On the
contrary, the popular mentality, to the extent that it considers
images at all, would tend to see them as copies of the physical
world that can be used or dismissed at will.

Such an interpretation, in part at least, was the thrust of the
earliest reflection in Western culture. The Greeks such as
Heraclitus, Democritus, the Epicureans, and the Stoics had
basically the same starting point as the popular mentality of
today—the external world impressed images on the human

mind. From their perspective, once the impression was made, the images were translated into the categories of the soul. Windelband, in discussing Democritus, explains how impressions, once they were received by the individual, set in motion the organs and through them the fire atoms of the soul.[9]

For the early Greeks, therefore, images were copies of the external world. In a materialistic system of thought such as that of Democritus, this determined character of human perception is not too difficult to appreciate. But certainly in Plato's system, with its doctrine of ideas and its emphasis on the incorporeal world, the human act of knowing is quite different. In fact, there is a different stress, but it is not easy to surface. The relationship between the perception and the knowledge of the higher forms is complex and, as Gulley points out, takes different turns in Plato's writings. Gulley sees the most complete treatment of sensible images in the *Timaeus*, and there he maintains that "the sensible world is an 'image' of the eternal."[10] Thus the perceptions one achieves can be helpful in knowing the Forms. In the continuum of Greek thought, therefore, Plato conceives a different goal for images, but he still stresses the formative impact of the senses.

Aristotle also remains within the mainstream tradition of Greek thinking about images. One's initial perception still is not seen as primarily interpretive. But Aristotle does show some departure from the tradition in that he gives a more creative role to human consciousness. He attributes to the workings of the human mind a common sense that mediates between the animal soul and the peculiar human soul. It is in this activity that one finds some creativity in the human imaging process. Brett puts it in the following terms:

As the process of sensation actualizes or gives form to the sense-faculty, an image is primarily the effect of the external stimulus, and regarded in abstraction from its source may be called an image or presentation. Representation, or the reproduction of the image in the absence of the original stimulus, is imagination. By virtue of these inner movements, which are psychic, man is able to store up and reproduce many images, and one image may be the cause of another, or more correctly one movement may set up a movement which previously occurred in some relation with it.[11]

The key, of course, to Aristotle's innovation is what Brett terms the "inner movements." Through the mediating common sense one is able to give creative combinations to images. Such innovation has obvious potential for the human thought process.

There are, therefore, major differences among Democritus, Plato, and Aristotle. They are agreed, however, on the strong formative influence of the physical world on our initial image. This is not the case with the early Christian thinkers. While they show an indebtedness to the Greek tradition, their peculiar concerns had an effect on their presentation of the human thought process. Klinger speaks of two such concerns: the stress on the freedom of the will and the spiritualization of the immortal soul.[12]

In their desire to stress the freedom and inviolability of the person, the early Christian writers instinctively ignored any essential connection between the outer material world and the inner developments of the soul. All psychological activities, including the world of images, were placed in the inner person. Thus, Augustine, the most influential of the early Christian thinkers, was ingenious in the introspective grasp of the self that he had. But he was all but silent in commenting on how the self draws from the outer world. In speaking of imagination, he places it as a mediating faculty "between memory and understanding, not between sense and memory."[13] Unlike reason, the imagination is limited to sense images, but it is pictured as an active faculty in contrast to earlier emphasis on its passive nature.

The struggle of these early thinkers thus shows the dynamics that face anyone dealing with the question of images. What is the influence of the external world on the internal? What is the nature of the sense impression? Is the extent of its impression determinative, as many of the Greek thinkers would have it, or are there innate thinking powers that operate more or less independently of the sensate world, as the early Christian writers thought? In short, does the external world impress images on the mind or are images creative responses to the reality one experiences?

It would be ignorant, of course, to say that the history of thought has shown no deviation from the basic positions taken by those who have laid the foundation of Western thinking. Aquinas, John of Salisbury, and the nominalists had their points of view which any treatment of the history of human thought must consider. But they worked within the general dynamics of their predecessors. With some there is a stress on the formative influence of the physical world; with others, an emphasis on the creative independence of the individual.

A similar dynamic is found in modern considerations. If any single characteristic would set the modern period in contrast to more traditional presentations, however, it would be a greater resistance to collapsing the tension in either direction. On the one hand, the conclusion of modern psychological studies is not compatible with the position of the early Greek thinkers that presented human perception as a means of recording copies of the outer world. There is an overwhelming amount of evidence which insists that acts of perception are classified according to categories of perception.

In practical terms such a stance insists that objects are perceived as having roundness or squareness. They are grouped in parallels and placed in fields of perception. Colors, likewise, are structured and categorized differently by different persons. From a psychological point of view an individual brings a personal history to each act of perception. As one gazes at a cluster of clouds one can organize them into elephants, cars, frying pans, crosses, or arrangements of flowers. What is seen depends on the dynamics of the person.

Likewise, the overwhelming evidence from a physiological perspective supports the interpretive quality of human perception. On the simplest grounds one could argue how the normal eye records the outer world one way while the abnormal eye records it another. In either case, whether one is arguing from a psychological or a physiological perspective, the outer world is not seen in a purely objective way.

On the other hand, however, a modern stance cannot accept the position of the early Christian thinkers. Given the modern experience, it is simply impossible to see the human as independent of the outer physical world. The human lives in a complex environment and is in constant dialogue with its surroundings. There are in fact few burning attacks on the importance of the physical world for human thought. Henry H. Price strongly emphasizes this point in his work *Thinking and Experience*. He argues that there are Realists, who emphasize universals as being "abstracted from real objects"; Conceptualists, who hold abstract ideas as "founded on the similitude of things"; and Imagists, who insist that thought is, in the words of Locke, *"cum fundamente in re."*[14] All, however, note the origin of thought in the objects of the world.

In modern thinking, therefore, the tension between the inner and outer origin of images is generally maintained. Descartes, for example, even with his strong emphasis on the mechanical workings of the physical body, still maintained the duality of soul and body since he was unwilling to reduce the inner workings of the human to the outer structure. Like most of the early pioneers of the scientific movement, he has a basic stance on the uniqueness of the interior of life that he is unwilling to sacrifice. Kantor offers an interesting comment on these early scientific thinkers:

The division of nature in the history of science is a definite outcome of the fact that while the early modern scientists concerned themselves with particular things and events, they were all at the same time dominated by transcendent traditions. Thus, they invented the dichotomic doctrines of spirit and matter, of the objective and subjective, of primary and secondary qualities, and of noumena and phenomena. It is an established fact that the great heroes of modern science were mystics and theologians. Call off the list: Copernicus, Kepler, Descartes, Galileo, Boyle, Newton. It is true enough that not all of these have overtly declared their theological interests, but that is only incidental.[15]

Kantor's point may be well taken. Perhaps the leaders of early science were dominated by "transcendent traditions." But certainly for modern thinkers one cannot suggest a similar domination. However, one does find in the literature and in the debates of today the same tension between an inner creativity and an outer determination. Klinger captures the persistence of the debate in the following terms:

Since Aristotle, and especially since Augustine, ideation has been regarded as some sort of positive activity under the individual's control. Aristotle and Hobbes have stated with particular clarity their conviction that thought is of at least two different minds, one with little voluntary direction, and the other voluntary and directed. This distinction, which has persisted, for instance, in sharp distinctions between primary and secondary process (Freud, 1900), autistic and directed thinking (Berlyne, 1965), or A-thinking and R-thinking (McKellar, 1957), will form an important part of the present analysis.[16]

There is then a dialogue taking place between the individual and the "others" encountered. On the one hand, such a dialogue clearly insists that one cannot see, hear, taste, smell, or feel exactly what one wants unless one has withdrawn completely from the dialogue. On the other hand, one must arrange and select that which will be perceived, and this act is interpretive. It is an interpretation that one does not form at will but which draws from the cultural synthesis in which one lives. This synthesis in turn is a complex of postures solidified from the dominant experiences of a culture. Thus, what was once seen as the mind "receiving, combining, and reproducing" images is now seen as a process of "selecting, grouping, and restructuring,"[17]

Images are, then, a basic way that the human has for interpreting the world. Such a statement would seem to be well within the major tradition of Western thought. One can start with Aristotle in his work *On Memory and Recollection* where he argues that one cannot begin to think without the use of mental images and then continue to a modern study such as Klinger's that surveys the psychological literature. He states: "most periods of consciousness can be confidently asserted to contain images, but the possibility of imageless periods cannot be ruled out."[18] Thus one can see why the types of images one has will have an impact on all the dynamics of human thought. But no issue that reaches into the complexity of the mind can admit of such a simple solution.

Those who would wish to dismiss images, or at least lessen their importance, approach the subject from many perspectives. On the simplest level one can find those who acknowledge the importance of spatial orientation but deny that such a starting point must have its roots in images. Wittgenstein argues, for example, that other spatial and physical representations such as charts, diagrams, or scaled models might serve a similar function.[19]

On a more serious level there are those who would not deny the existence of images in thought, but dismiss such thought as characteristic of the less profound, less important part of human consciousness. Words and the more demanding dynamics of abstract thinking would be considered the most important human activity. This would seem to be either the

implied or explicit position of many modern philosophers who
ignore the question of images entirely or who give it only passing consideration.

Perhaps incorrectly, Heidegger is singled out by some as
representing this tradition. One finds such a statement as the
following:

> Language is not a mere tool, one of the many which man
> possesses; on the contrary, it is only language that affords
> the very possibility of standing in the openness of the exis-
> tent. Only where there is language is there world.[20]

In commenting on Heidegger's search Funk notes that "he
essays to track the metaphysical tradition in the West to the
soil out of which it sprang. And that soil is language
understood as the place where being comes to dwell."[21] The
language that Heidegger is promoting is, of course, that of the
living metaphorical utterance over the analytical dead
language that uses words as lifeless instruments. Put within
the context of his work as a whole, therefore, and given the
poetic flow of his writing, it would be difficult to argue any intention of excluding images from the inner workings of human
consciousness. But clearly images as such are not emphasized.

Finally, there are those who attack the use of the term "image" itself. Perhaps this approach can be best represented by
Sartre. We find him dismissing the entire literature that Klinger
surveys:

> Yet we shall unearth this naïve ontology of images as a
> more or less implicit postulate of all the psychologists who
> have studied the subject. All, or almost all, have committed
> the confusion noted earlier between identity of essence and
> identity of existence.[22]

Earlier Sartre had characterized this "naïve ontology of images" as insisting that an image is a "lesser thing" and is pres-

ent to one's awareness "like any other thing" and is still in some way attached to "the things of which it is the image." He sees this idea of a "thing-image" as coming from the "great metaphysicians of the past."

> Descartes, Leibniz, and Hume had one and the same conception of the image. They ceased to agree only when they went on to consider the relation of image to thoughts.[23]

In essence Sartre is attacking the position started by the Greeks. He may be aware of certain improvements that Descartes, Leibniz, and Hume have made on the tradition, but he feels that the basic thrust is the same. He is clearly arguing for a more creative projection to the imaging process. Images are not primarily passive responses to outward stimuli, no matter how creative one makes such activity. Rather, they are active projections of the assertive individual in its attempt to create. Thus, one can find Sartre in a sense dismissing the term itself:

> There is no avoiding the straightforward answer that so long as images are inert psychic contents, there is no conceivable way to reconcile them with the requirements of synthesis. . . . Rather, an image is *a certain type of consciousness*. An image is an act, not some thing. An image is a consciousness *of* some thing.[24]

Sartre obviously does not deny the impact of the physical environment on one's inner space. He is not simply repeating the tradition of some of the earlier Christian thinkers. He is, instead, presenting a rather subtle but important fresh perspective on the entire controversy. Certainly the material world must be dealt with, but every image is an action. It is "a certain type of consciousness." And it takes place as the individual interacts with the physical world in an attempt to synthesize and create in the world. Price puts the argument in the following terms:

There is the imaging, and the thing imaged, and there is no intermediate entity ('an image') coming between them. What we image is just a house or a dog or a sound or perhaps a smell. And this is not something immaterial and private and intra mental. It is something physical and public.[25]

Of the three points of objection, the last presents the greatest difficulty to this work. The initial argument of this volume asserted that images are interpretive spatial arrangements in response to acts of perception and as such serve as a starting point for verbal articulation. To make such a claim is not to accept what Price terms a strict Imagist position. He describes that approach in the following way:

Mental images are the primary symbols, and all other symbols are secondary symbols. Of course, the Imagist does not deny that words have meaning, but he holds that they have it only indirectly, as substitutes for images.[26]

The present argument, it is true, gives an important place to images; insists that the greater part of human thought employs them; but it does not hold that words have meaning "only indirectly" or "as substitutes for images." Do words give rise to images or are images always required for words? That is a futile inquiry for which extensive psychological testing or intense reflection on our experiences cannot give a compelling answer. Rather, the important point is that all of human thought is interrelated. The words one uses will have an impact on how one reacts to moments of experience. Conversely, the types of images one forms in response to stimuli will have an impact on one's verbalization. Thus images are important for religious reflection at any level.

The present approach can accept, therefore, the first two cautions about images; namely, that some thought is imageless or that some can employ other forms of spatial orientation provided one accepts the basic unity of human reflection.

It would have more difficulty with the third position, however. There is admittedly some danger in speaking of images in terms of entities or particulars. They are not simple reproductions or pictures that are stored. They are active responses to internal and external stimuli. But any intelligent use of the term must acknowledge that something is produced. As fascinating as Sartre's approach may at first appear, it must finally be rejected or at least corrected as an overstatement. There is a middle ground between what he terms "inert psychic contents" and rejecting the use of any noun to describe this activity of human consciousness. Using Price's terms, there is "an image" and one is not simply "imaging" the outer world. Not to reject Sartre's position would in fact restrict the very creativity that he wants to promote, for his position seems to restrict human consciousness too rigidly to the forms of the world.

One should realize, of course, that the content or the entity called "image" is not stored in some chamber of human memory to be called forth as situations demand. Rather, each act of perception or experience will produce an image-making response. The images produced will be similar to and dependent on those present in the past history of the person involved, but they will not be duplications. Put in slightly different terms, one never simply remembers. One remembers with a purpose, and the purpose influences how something is remembered.

Human thought has both a continuity and a creativity. It also has a unity and a complexity. Neither of these tensions should be collapsed. Out of the first tension one maintains what Price terms the "private and intra mental" as well as rejects with Sartre the "inert psychic contents." Out of the second tension one recognizes the projecting action of images as well as the informative impact of the physical world without denying a single term for both activities. In emphasizing the projecting activity of human awareness, one may be more intent on exploring possibilities rather than measuring one's consciousness by the structures and forms of the physical world as it is presently known. On the other hand, in emphasizing the passive gesture of human consciousness, one may be more intent on grasping the physical world as it is encountered by the common senses. But intentions do not change the medium. One can use images for many different purposes. But it would only confuse one's grasp of human awareness to multiply categories to meet intentions.

At this point, then, this work will argue three points. First, the image is the medium used in most human thought. Second, given the unity of all human consciousness, even thought not directly dependent on images will be affected by the tone and awareness that images create in the person. And finally, given the argument that will be developed in the second chapter, that film is a medium of images which occupies one fourth of the average person's waking hours, one must realize that the medium will have a tremendous impact on consciousness in general and religious awareness in particular.

Imaginative Constructs

Image making is, therefore, a primary human activity. The simplest and most useless statement that could be made about the origins of images is that they are produced by the imagination. The statement is useless because the use of the term "imagination" clearly shows that no single word has so successfully defied definition. As late as the nineteenth century one finds people such as Coleridge speaking of it as a special faculty of human knowing. But such clear divisions of human activity seem contrary to the present-day realization that concepts such as "the imagination" are abstractions erected to make one aware of the different activities of a very complex whole termed, among other things, "human consciousness." Simply put, humans are aware that they produce images and that they are able to image encounters in very different ways. Thus they give this activity a separate name and in their less exact moods speak of it as a separate thing or faculty. They name the activity or faculty the imagination.

One's attitude toward this activity or faculty also admits of many movements. When one wants to express dissatisfaction with the precision and detail of a presentation, a ready phrase is available, "It leaves much to the imagination." The contention is, of course, that more exactness, detail, or precision would be conducive to insight, truth, or awareness than the simply suggestive. Imagination in this context is given the connotation of a vagueness that leaves one floundering.

Extending even further into the negative end of the continuum of attitudes, the imagination can be given a Walter Mitty embodiment as an escape from reality. One who can no longer handle the societal pressures withdraws into a world of simple fabrication—an enclosure that protects against the crushing demands from without. This projection can, of course, be countered by the positive side, where the imagination can be seen as the only way the human has of dealing with reality. Faced with the material world humans realize that they are swimming in a mysterious milieu. They do not know what it is. They cannot know what it is in any complete sense. It is beyond human capabilities to grasp fully that of which they are a part. The most one can do is to probe that which is encountered through means of symbols and systems of symbols.

To insist that one does not know reality in its fullness does not reduce human awareness to a quandary of simple subjectivity. It is only to state that the human task is to probe for insight through that which it encounters. The imagination is the starting point for any such probing. When one speaks of truth, therefore, the question should be how much insight does a particular way of approaching reality offer. To borrow

a term from Gerard Manley Hopkins, one can counter the
negative end of the continuum by asking on the positive end
how much *inscape* does a particular approach offer.

To situate the phrase, "It leaves much to the imagination,"
at the positive end of the continuum would be to stress that a
particular approach opens up new avenues of insight, new
ways of putting concrete and abstract experiences together. It
may offer new ways of organizing symbols or even offer new
symbols.

From what has been said about images in the previous section it should be obvious that this volume assumes a positive
attitude toward imagination. It will argue forcefully that not
only are humans continually imaging events and encounters in
an attempt to digest them, but that they extend this spatial
orientation to life as a whole. They produce basic imaginative
constructs that attempt to orient their lives in sweeping terms.
In comparison to images these imaginative constructs are not
an essentially different human activity. The difference is more
in terms of intention or goals. Where images are generally in
response to immediate situations, imaginative constructs are
geared more toward absorbing direction as a whole. Like the
images of the previous section, these constructs are essential
for human reflection. Both are essentially the same activity—orienting the human spatially.

Where this volume uses the term "imaginative construct" to
suggest the continuity with the previous section, William F.
Lynch would speak of paradigms for human understanding
and Ian T. Ramsey would develop the idea of model. All intend to show that the imagination attempts to set the field of
human consciousness in which activities such as conception
and perception are placed. Such a statement is not meant to
present imagination in a tyrannical relationship with the more
particular acts of human knowing, for it must remain in
dialogue with them in the same way that images emerge from
the dialogue between the individual and the world of objects.

But these imaginative constructs are very important for all facets of human knowing.

Lynch tries to suggest the extent of their importance when he quotes this passage from Norwood Russell Hanson's *Patterns of Discovery*:

> Let us consider Johannes Kepler: imagine him on a hill watching the dawn. With him is Tycho Brahe. Kepler regarded the sun as fixed: it was the earth that moved. But Tycho followed Ptolemy and Aristotle in this much at least: the earth was fixed and all other celestial bodies moved around it. Do Kepler and Tycho see the same thing in the east at dawn?[27]

Actually the point Lynch tries to make may be taken a step further in that those educated today see all bodies moving in relation to all other bodies. Or do they picture the event this way? Here precisely is the difference between a conception and the imaginative framework of an individual. Most educated individuals would be able to offer the highly relational answer when pressed for "exactness." But in their everyday life, most picture the earth going around the sun. Furthermore, the astronomer would insist that all three constructs are hypotheses that account for the relationship. The latter, highly relational one is preferred simply because it accounts for the observable relationships in the simplest way. Thus, none of the three hypotheses grasps things as they really are; nor does one's conception necessarily dictate one's ordinary perception. This example demonstrates in some measure what is meant by the term "imaginative construct" as it applies to human knowledge.

One more example would press the point, for it is important. The vast majority of people educated in the West accept the concepts of molecules and atoms. According to the kinetic theory out of which these concepts grew, all the objects are composed of less than one-percent matter. What matter that is there is in frantic motion, and the matter itself is seen as energy in a temporary state of stability. While this may be a hypothesis of the world that many are willing to accept, it is not the way many sense the world. They are more content to see a world of things. If this conception were to seep into the marrow of their bones to the extent that they would sense the world as event, they would be presented with a radically different context in which to picture the human situation. The scientist's reply to these imaginings would have to be, however, that neither picture captures the world as it is. The most one can argue is that one way of viewing may cause more insight than the other. Such a judgment is just that—a judgment—and not an obvious conclusion. It may, however, be a very compelling judgment.

The imagination then measures itself against the world as it is known. It may creatively play with the arrangements of what is known, but it always measures itself by what is culturally acceptable if not accepted. As a matter of fact, the imagination in most people is conservative. The individual as well as a culture works within a mind set that grows out of a dominant experience. One will notice that the examples used above were from the scientific world. The reason is obvious: science is the dominant experience of the twentieth century in Western culture and as such dominates its cultural imagination. For the present one can simply note that in many primitive cultures, literature and myths are dominated by cyclic imagery. This can be accounted for in part by the lack in primitive cultures of noticeable linear change and in part by their being overwhelmed by the cycle of seasons which dominates their lives as herdsmen or farmers.

Such statements as these are simplified to emphasize the point. Western culture, which has experienced such linear change largely through the workings of science, is limited in the way it can picture reality. Given the input of culture on the individual, no one in the present setting can very easily picture the world in a cyclic way. This is not to say that no such individuals exist. For the individual can have pressing experiences of his or her own that radically alter the composite of conscious existence. There is also the important creative action of the will on an individual's conscious life.

Stories

Speaking of images and imaginative constructs as basic human responses to the encounters of life may appear to be strange. Not too many are aware that they are dominated by spatial interpretations despite a strong consensus among those who examine human ways of knowing. But a further step is necessary for human knowing, and it may not appear to be quite so strange as some of the previous discussion. Humans must take these abstracted responses of images and imaginative constructs and give them flesh and bones. They must incorporate them into more immediate recognizable movements which this study will term "stories." They must have stories about what their life is and what should or could be. This is all part of the process by which persons identify and confront.

In an article about television violence George Gerbner and Larry Gross pick up on this need for stories and television's role in producing life stories:

> Common rituals and mythologies are agencies of symbolic socialization and control. They demonstrate how society works by dramatizing its norms and values. They are essential parts of the general system of messages that cultivates prevailing outlooks (which is why we call it culture) and regulates social relationships. This system of messages, with its story-telling function, makes people perceive as real and normal and right that which fits established social order.[28]

Gerbner and Gross are, of course, speaking of how a society must function by creating stories that "dramatize its norms and values." But the same is true for individuals. They must work out the issues of the self in dramatic forms, not necessarily to fit some established order but to establish some emotional order or integration. This is evident in the free-flowing stories of their fantasy life.

Klinger speaks of fantasies as "response sequences," which, of course, has been the way of looking at the most active type of fantasy stories—sleep dreams. While one's sleep dreams are noted for their deviation from societal reality, they deal with the basic issues of one's person placed in that reality. As one is associating people, places, and events from childhood with those of later life, there is no question that the impacts dealt with are basic. The issues of one's person are too great to be dealt with on a simple rational level. One cannot effect the releases and integrations necessary by proceeding through measured procedures that trim the expression to the logical categories. A freer, open forum is necessary. Just as mentally ill persons must withdraw from societal reality because they have dimensions which they are unable to express in restrictive frameworks, so all humans must be given some outlet for free expression. A healthy insane life while asleep is necessary for a healthy sane life while awake.

But this type of story is just one aspect of the entire picture. One's fantasies are not always so bizarre. Most are rather mundane. One can look at daydreams in which there is a more conscious control over one's psychic life. Like the more exotic sleep dreams, these mental activities are responses and therefore offer a positive contribution to one's person. Singer gives the positive tone that he tried to nurture in his book *Daydreaming*:

Previous chapters have emphasized the function of daydreaming as either a natural feature of development or as a potential skill available for practice and adaptive use. Such an emphasis has been intentional in order to counteract the more widely held view of fantasy as a defensive maneuver or symptom of severe maladjustment or schizoid tendencies.[29]

The purpose of this section does not allow extended development of the point, but the potential that Singer suggests for daydreams serves also as the impetus for the emphasis in psychological and religious movements on all types of stories including psychodramas and biographies. All are seen as openings for the expressions of dimensions not able to be dealt with on a simply rational level. While the responses are not consciously measured, they are responses to both the inward and outward forces that stir the center. Like the more abstract activities of the imagination, the story form is basically working with immediate encounters. It therefore builds upon the primary encounter with the world of objects.

Religious Consciousness and the Imagination

The previous sections affirm the following positions:

1. Human consciousness receives stimulation from perception. These perceptions are interpretive acts that result from the interplay of the object and the individual's dominant categories of perceiving.

2. Images are efferent responses to acts of perception and memories of perceptions that grow out of the dialogue of a complex of human mental activities.

3. Imagination is a type of mental activity that produces an imagery field for all acts of knowing. Its relation to other forms of human knowing is not tyrannical but dialogic.

4. Abstract spatial orientations such as images and imaginative constructs must be further concretized into story forms.

The question now arises as to what role these functions play in the development of religious consciousness. The problem of definitions is no less difficult here than in other sections. It is a problem common to the use of all words that are a part of a popular vocabulary. Just as "image," "imagination," and "story" are used in many different senses, so the term "religious" finds a wide spectrum of meaning. Even academic uses of the term present no simple common ground. The list of phrases is long—"ultimate concern" (Tillich), "feeling of dependence" (Schleiermacher), "sense of the sacred" (Otto), "noetic integrator" (Huxley).

To some extent, of course, the thrust of one's definition is governed by the context in which it appears. Ronald R. Cavanagh, for example, offers the following definition: "Religion is the varied, symbolic expression of, and appropriate response to, that which people deliberately affirm as being of unrestricted value to them."[30] Such a definition intends to be as inclusive as possible without sacrificing clarity. But it is a definition found in a general introduction to religion. As such there is no attempt to promote one approach to life as more insightful than another. Secondly, Cavanagh is concentrating on religion and not religious consciousness. Thus he speaks of "symbolic expression of, and appropriate response to." Religion, in other words, as distinguished from religious consciousness deals with the communal or individual response to some dynamic present in the individual. This present study, in contrast, is concentrating on the inner dynamics and not the outward ritual expression. Such a division is unfortunate, of course. But the demand for a focus to any study insists that some clustering of the human complex be made. To the extent, therefore, that Cavanagh's definition highlights the idea of religion as active expression and to the extent that he does not intend critically to promote a point of view, his definition would prove inadequate for the present study.

In contrast, this work in its introductory remarks has already promoted several specific views about the human quest that it must take into account in formulating its working definition of religious consciousness. To begin with, the human is seen in continual dialogue with the world of others. It is true that the individual and collective consolidations of the self and society present necessary points of reference as the human seeks some perspective on the flood of experience, but finally the persistent dialogue will challenge these consolidations and the human will move to new perspectives. The human can never shut itself off from the challenge of others; the human will never rest easily in one permanent perspective.

The implications of this first stance will, therefore, place the work in tension with many modern approaches to religious awareness which stress the psychological effects rather than the causes of such effects. Some definitions in this cluster border on the simplistic. John Dewey, for example, states in his work *A Common Faith*:

> The actual religious quality in the experience described is the *effect* produced, the better adjustment in life and its conditions, not the manner and cause of its production. The way in which the experience operated, its function, determines its religious value.[31]

Other definitions are much more subtle and sensitive about the power and uniqueness of the religious experience. But they still put too much stress on the subjective element. Rudolph Otto takes Schleiermacher to task for this very reason:

> The religious category discovered by him, by whose means he professes to determine the real content of the religious emotion, is merely a category of self-evaluation, in the sense of self-depreciation. According to him the religious emotion would be directly and primarily a sort of self-consciousness, a feeling concerning oneself in a special,

determined relation, viz. one's dependence. Thus, according to Schleiermacher, I can only come upon the very fact of God as the result of an inference, that is, by reasoning to a cause beyond myself to account for my "feeling of dependence."[32]

Given the dynamics of human knowing that have been laid down in the opening sections of this work, Otto's reservations are appreciated. Likewise, Donald D. Evans is also appreciated when he protests against those who work out of Tillich's depth experience and make too simple an equation of such an experience with the religious experience.

> I . . . wish to distinguish my account of religious faith from some which resemble it in taking a depth-experience seriously and in finding common ground between believers and some unbelievers, but which differ in equating a depth-experience with faith or with God.[33]

To this point, therefore, this chapter has insisted that the human is continually in dialogue with others and rejects any approach that gives too much stress to the subjective. Likewise, in its discussion of human reflection, it has resisted any tendency to divide human reflection into many and varied compartments. There is a complexity, true. But human reflection must be grasped in its wholeness. Therefore, in developing any working definition of religious consciousness, this volume will reject any tendency to associate religious consciousness with one faculty of human knowing. Joachim Wach notes such movements in the following grid:

> From Schleiermacher to James, Whitehead, and Otto it was sought in feeling; from Hegel and Martineau to Brightman, in the intellect; and from Fichte to Reinhold Niebuhr, in the will.[34]

Wach may be overstating his case when he dismisses "the tiresome discussion." But certainly Marrett and Allport were correct in their work with the term "religious" when the first states "in any such concrete phase, processes of thinking, feeling and willing are alike involved"[35] and the latter holds that the religious experience "must be viewed as an indistinguishable blend of emotion and reason, of feeling and meaning."[36]

One other point must be noted. This human whole that is in dialogue with the world of others has its basic stimulation in its physical encounters. Such a position would seem implied in the previous emphasis on dialogue, but it is important for a work focusing on film to insist that basic to that dialogue is contact with the world of physical objects. It is particularly important because there are religious positions that would clearly oppose such a stance. Thus Karl Barth would have little patience with such a study when he wrote the following passage:

> There is no room for revelation in the Christian sense in any human inquiry or any human faculty of reason. And the same applies to what we have called God in the Christian sense. . . . And so we must say that if a purely human conception of the world is the measure of all things, then neither revelation nor God in the Christian sense exist at all. We would in fact have been speaking of "nothing" when we were speaking about revelation and God.[37]

In contrast to such a statement, the position taken here insists that experience and reflection on that experience is the starting place. Knowledge of any dimension starts from this reference. It is upon this contention that the whole association of film and the religious dimension is based.

To this point, then, several requirements for a working definition of religious consciousness have been established. It must stress the experience that the self has of the world of others and not simply describe the psychological movements of the individual, for the self is in dialogue with the world and not simply turned inwards. Secondly, the definition must present the wholeness of the human response and not locate the religious dimension in any single faculty. And finally, by its very nature, the human draws from its contact with the physical world. Added to these dynamics about the human struggle, then, two more preliminary questions about focus will be stressed. First, what is the specific focus of religious reflection as distinguished from other forms of reflection? Second, what terms or words can be used to address this focus?

In dealing with the first concern there will be no attempt to retract what has been said about human wholeness. But when one is using a concept such as "religious" one must be precise, for this is what the form of human reflection called "conceptualization" demands. To use the term in too vague a sense would weaken the challenge of the work. Likewise, to give too narrow a definition would unnecessarily restrict its application. Neither direction is desirable for an interdisciplinary work such as this.

As a starting position, then, it can be noted that most uses of the term "religious" insist that it is an extraordinary sense of reality. They generally insist that what appears to be a world of multiplicities is in fact radically related. Some positions might argue that the multiplicities are in fact one. But at the very least religious consciousness must insist that there is a basic relatedness to what appears to the common sense to be a world of distinct and separate entities. This relatedness has its foundation in a common source, a greater whole that grounds, generates, nurtures, or sustains the individual existences, including human existence. That which causes other life causes human life.

What is obvious, of course, is that the extent to which one is dealing with an extraordinary sense of reality, one that challenges the common sense, language will not be easy. The terms for the greater whole one finds in contemporary writings vary greatly: God, Existence, Being, Life Force, Ground of Being, and Presence. Each of the terms, especially in their varied contexts, are arguing for different aspects. Even a given term such as "God" has many different meanings within a common religious heritage. A Christian theologian speaking from a traditional notion of God presents quite a different view than one working from the same religious tradition but through a process system of thought.

One cannot, then, make simple equations between the given terms or between different contexts for a single term. But once the caution is raised, one must counter it by insisting that there are major similarities among most religious reflections. There is usually some emphasis on the relatedness of all in reference to the one greater whole. Thus one finds Otto describing the objects of religious consciousness in the following terms: "Something that is at once absolutely supreme in power and reality and wholly non-rational."[38]

On a more personal note he goes on to quote William James:

> The perfect stillness of the night was thrilled by a more solemn silence. The darkness held a presence that was all the more felt because it was not seen. I could not any more have doubted that *He* was there than that I was. Indeed, I felt myself to be, if possible, the less real of the two.[39]

Perhaps most religious experiences are not so intense as that of James's that one senses the reality of the other more than oneself. But there is the other that is experienced. It is a dialogue of one's being with what Evans too simply terms "God," with what Otto describes as something that is "absolutely supreme in power and reality and wholly non-rational" and with what James terms "a presence that was all the more felt because it was not seen."

To this point, then, the preliminary questions have been articulated. The presuppositions of the earlier sections have been restated and the peculiar focus of religious consciousness has been developed. The working definition can now be for-

mulated: Religious consciousness is the sense of relatedness
that the human has with the others of the world as all are
rooted in a common greater whole. Such a definition does capture the total human responding to its experience of that
which nurtures all forms of existence encountered in and
through the physical world. These were the basic criteria that
the study had established to this point.

Before turning attention to the specific relationship of
religious consciousness and imagination, however, a final
word about terms will be helpful. At various points in this
study different phrases will be used to capture the unique
potential of film in sensitizing individuals to what is here called
the "greater whole." In a given context the term "life force"
may be used when there is a stress on the living dynamic of the
greater whole—a dynamic that film as an art of moving
pictures is espcially adept at capturing. In another context a
term such as "Being" may be chosen because film is also a
medium that has its origins in individual shots. To some
extent, then, it captures and preserves isolated expressions as
they existed in a period of time. The phrases and terms, in
other words, will vary as different aspects of the greater whole
are stressed.

With the working definition formulated, therefore, attention must now focus on the specific relation of religious consciousness and imagination. The connection between the two
should not be too difficult to grasp since the imagination has
been presented as the interpretive backdrop in which humans
place all their knowing. Thus, one's imaginative framework
will determine whether a religious consciousness is possible
and what type of religious consciousness will be maintained.
If one sees the world as separate entities, as a collection of
things, there then seems little soil in which a religious consciousness can take hold. If, on the other hand, one sees the
world as guided by invisible spirits, then the possibilities of a
religious consciousness are fertile, though only a certain type
of religious consciousness. The key here is that one starts with

organizing constructs (not necessarily one) into which all one's seeing and knowing are fed.

The imagination is, therefore, the backdrop of human consciousness. But it must be remembered that the imagination always remains in dialogue with the world of experience. This is why imaginations change. Thus, when science began to show the cause of change in the physical structure of things, it became more and more difficult to picture the world as governed by invisible spirits. If a loved one is stricken with cancer, the cultural experience today may cause one's line of thought to picture the following: heavy smoking, a chemical reaction in the body, a virus developing from this imbalance, the resulting undisciplined growth of cells. It would only be despite the cultural experience that one could picture a God in human terms deciding which individual shall be cursed and which shall be cured.

Imagination can, of course, act in such a way. In point of fact, many—although immersed in a scientific world view—will also work with simple anthropomorphic images. One is not dealing with the strictness of conceptual logic. The imagination can focus on a variety of models that include in themselves a variety of human convictions. But since imagination measures itself against the culturally acceptable, some paradigms are more acceptable than others. Mention has already been made of the difficulty for the modern mind to picture a cyclic context. Similarly, any romantic vision of nature in a deified form would have to undergo radical revisions for one exposed to the technological experience and the dominant presence of the human in all sectors of the world.

In one sense of the term, "faith," then, may be equated with imagination. The way persons organize and structure external and internal movements expresses their basic orientation toward the world. This is what Lynch seems to be driving at in the following passage:

Faith, I am suggesting, has a similar relationship to the world; it provides a structure or a context. It is a way of experiencing and imagining the world: or it is a world within which we experience or imagine. It composes it or, if you will, it recomposes the world according to its terms. For example, the beatitudes totally recompose ordinary appearance. To believe that the poor are *blessed* puts an entirely different light on things.[40]

There is, of course, another dimension to faith that this use of the term does not embody; namely, the convinced stance in the face of overwhelmingly contradictory evidence. History is filled with incidences of individuals who would not be budged in their convictions despite all reasonable arguments. These figures often emerge as attractive heroes or heroines. They exercise an appeal, especially if they are proven right. Does this equation of imagination and faith make any sense in the face of such examples? If so, what can one say of the dialogic character of the imagination argued in the previous sections?

Put in slightly different terms the questions ask whether a faith can be by its very nature dialogic and whether an imagination can be committed. In answering the latter it has already been noted that most imaginations are conservative. There is, therefore, a tendency to hold on to a given way of envisioning. Imagination may not have the conscious purpose of preserving the governing images, imaginative constructs, and life stories. But there is enough desire for permanence in the human soul that something akin to commitment can be found in the dynamics of the imagination.

In answering the first part of the inquiry—can one equate faith and imagination?—one must discuss some of the peculiarities facing the modern religious consciousness. Certainly faith has as one of its movements a sense of commitment. Given a set of dynamics in a given culture, commitment may become the dominant movement and the object of commitment may be highly consolidated and self-assured. But faith also prompts an openness and a trust. Given another set of dynamics in a given culture, these may become the dominant movement of a faith. The latter would seem to be the case of religious consciousness today.

Certainly this inclusion of the imagination in religious consciousness may appear strange to some. Certainly the equation of the two terms would seem foreign. In point of fact, when the dominant experience of a people has been digested and consolidated into a firm perspective, there would be little prompting to talk of the imagination. The imaginative context is so embedded in a people that they are not aware of it as a context. In such a situation there may be a significant number of secondary abstractions taking place which work out of the cultural presuppositions. Such has been the case at various points in the history of religious thought.

Such consolidation is not, of course, the situation today. The scientific experience and the resulting world of rapid linear change and technology have so radically challenged major cultural phantasms as to call forth a major effort by the collective imagination in order to allow some consolidation of human life. That present Western culture is disoriented in the face of overwhelming new experiences is such an accepted conclusion, it does not need debate.

What one must face in such a situation, however, is the possibilities of religious reflection. In a state of cultural consolidation or where revelation is seen as a body of particular truths, abstract reasoning processes about the nature of Being (theodicy) and the implications of such a Being for beings (theology) present an active and beneficial field. But faced with cultural confusion and the resulting view of revelation as at best general, traditional efforts of theology seem quite limited indeed. Culturally disoriented individuals must first consolidate their field of relationship with the life forces in such a way as to inform their dominant experiences. Until a culture is able to form a perspective on what is taking place in its life movements, secondary abstract thinking will be limited indeed. If the images of God, grace, and purpose have not developed from an assimilation of the dynamics of present human experience, secondary reflections that are derived from past assimilations will prove of limited value.

To make such a claim is not to dismiss past consolidations. They may indeed prove beneficial in the task that challenges the modern imagination. But even if Paul Ricoeur is correct in pointing to the possibility that archaic myths can be repossessed in some form by the present age, the modern imagination still must undertake substantial preparatory changes. Amos Wilder captures the task well in his book *Theopoetic*:

> Our argument has begun with the plea that Christian witness must engage our times at the level of its unconscious axioms and inherited symbolics and not only at that of its ideas. Since such cultural imagery is deep-rooted and powerful it can only be effectively encountered if Christianity draws on its own arsenal of vision. But this eloquence will not be persuasive unless it is lived out and unless its archetypes are quickened and reshaped in the encounter. Such encounter takes place in depth and at the public level.[41]

Wilder calls for a coming to grips with the "reality-sense," "the governing apperceptions," the "sensorium." At least in some sections of his work, Wilder presumes that these governing apperceptions are already present in some consolidated form. If such is the case, then the task is to surface and expand them so that they may be of greater use to our secondary reflection. If the case is otherwise, however, then the task for the imagination is to develop ways of assimilating the flood of experience.

In either situation the task calls for more attention being given to the symbolic and the prerational in religious reflection. This is what Wilder seems to refer to when he speaks of the theopoetic. It is what James Wiggins calls for when he says religious thought must depend more on aesthetics and ontology rather than reason and metaphysics.[42] Such a call does not ignore the importance of theology and the reasoning process. It simply calls attention to the pressing need to lay a new foundation for religious reflection today. Again, Amos Wilder addresses himself to the point:

> Before any new theologies however secular and radical there must be a contemporary theopoetic. The structures of faith and confession have always rested in hierophanies and images. But in each new age and climate the theopoetic of the church is reshaped in inseparable relation to the general imagination of the time.[43]

Within this context one can recognize the importance of the specific activities of the imagination. Encounters which challenge our images, imaginative constructs and life stories or suggest new ones such as the various visual and literary arts become exercises for the imagination that can lead to a definite growth in its awareness of that of which one is a part.

When one speaks of the religious consciousness, one is not dealing with a sense of the ordinary. The religious consciousness signifies an extraordinary sense of reality that apprehends the interrelatedness and perhaps the oneness of a creation that appears on first encounter to be multifaceted and separate. The religious consciousness must therefore thrust beyond the immediate sense of reality to an interpretive one.

To answer the question specifically, one would have to admit that the imagination and faith have certain dimensions that are included in one but not the other. The first seems to suggest an exploring activity that does not rule out commitment. The second would entail more commitment that does not rule out exploration. Since the two concepts cannot be simply equated, they should be preserved as separate terms. But given contemporary dynamics, the two overlap in an important way. It is this significant overlap which this volume wishes to explore within the movements of film.

Notes

1. Thomas Merton, *The Seven Storey Mountain* (Garden City: Garden City Books, 1951), p. 353.

2. Ibid., p. 22.

3. Ibid., p. 148.

4. Ibid., p. 149.

5. Ibid., p. 80.

6. Ibid., p. 149.

7. Media critics are correct in pointing out the differences between film and television. But the similarities are greater. We have used the term "film" to cover the vast overlap of the two media. The appendix will be used to suggest some important differences.

8. Thomas Gornall, "A Note on Imagination and Thought About God," in *A New Theology No. 1*, ed. Martin E. Marty and Dean G. Peerman (New York: Macmillan Company, 1964), p. 122.

9. Wilhelm Windelband, *A History of Philosophy* (New York: Harper and Brothers, 1958), p. 114.

10. Norman Gulley, *Plato's Theory of Knowledge* (London: Methuen and Co., 1962), p. 131.

11. R. S. Peters, ed., *Brett's History of Psychology* (New York: The Macmillan Company, 1962), p. 119.

12. Eric Klinger, *Structure and Functions of Fantasy* (New York: Wiley-Interscience, 1971), pp. 112-13.

13. Peters, p. 221.

14. H. H. Price, *Thinking and Experience* (London: Hutchinson University Library, 1969), p. 261.

15. J. R. Kantor, *The Scientific Evolution of Psychology* (Chicago: The Principia Press, Inc., 1963), p. 351.

16. Klinger, p. 115.

17. Peters, p. 694.

18. Klinger, p. 136.

19. Ludwig Wittgenstein, *Philosophical Investigations* (New York: The Macmillan Company, 1958). There are explicit as well as implicit statements throughout the work, e.g., the mid-five hundred section and the early six hundred.

20. Martin Heidegger, "Holderin and the Essence of Poetry," in *Existence and Being* (Chicago: Henry Regnery Company, 1949), pp. 299-300.

21. Robert W. Funk, *Language, Hermeneutic and Word of God* (New York: Harper & Row, 1966), p. 39.

22. Jean-Paul Sartre, *Imagination*, trans. Forrest Williams (Ann Arbor: University of Michigan Press, 1962), p. 5.

23. Ibid., p. 6.

24. Ibid., p. 146.

25. Price, p. 247.

26. Ibid., p. 239.

27. Norwood Russell Hanson, *Patterns of Discovery*, quoted in William F. Lynch, *Images of Faith* (Notre Dame: University of Notre Dame Press, 1973), p. 15.

28. George Gerbner and Larry Gross, "Living with Television: The Violence Profile," *Journal of Communication* 25 (Spring 1976): 173.

29. Jerome L. Singer, *Daydreaming* (New York: Random House, 1966), p. 194.

30. Ronald Cavanagh, "The Term Religion," in *Introduction to the Study of Religion*, ed. T. William Hall (New York: Harper & Row, 1978), p. 19.

31. John Dewey, *A Common Faith* (New Haven: Yale University Press, 1934), p. 14.

32. Rudolf Otto, *The Idea of the Holy* (New York: Oxford University Press, 1958), p. 10.

33. Donald D. Evans, "Difference Between Scientific and Religious Assertions," in *Science and Religion*, ed. Ian G. Barbour (New York: Harper & Row, 1968), p. 108.

34. Joachim Wach, *The Comparative Study of Religions*, ed. Joseph M. Kitagawa (New York: Columbia University Press, 1958), p. 33.

35. Robert R. Marrett, *The Threshold of Religion*, p. xxix, quoted in Kitagawa, *The Comparative Study of Religions*, p. 33.

36. Gordon Allport, *The Individual and His Religion*, pp. 16ff. quoted in Kitagawa, *The Comparative Study of Religions*, p. 34.

37. Karl Barth, *Against the Stream*, ed. Ronald Gregor Smith (New York: Philosophical Library, 1954), pp. 210-11.

38. Otto, p. 22.

39. Ibid., p. 66.

40. Lynch, p. 17.

41. Amos Wilder, *Theopoetics* (Philadelphia: Fortress Press, 1976), p. 29.

42. James B. Wiggins, "Within and Without Stories," in *Religion as Story*, ed. James B. Wiggins (New York: Harper & Row, 1975), p. 14.

43. Amos Wilder, *Grace Confounding: Poems*, quoted in *Theopoetics*, p. 1.

2

Images, the Medium, and Religious Consciousness

THE previous chapter spoke of "images" as interpretive acts that through the unity of human thought influence all our mental activities. It placed these images within the activity of the imagination, which also produces more general interpretive spatial orientations called "imaginative constructs." A third term was introduced, "story," to capture the human need to have these abstract spatial orientations embodied in more familiar, concrete situations. Finally, all three terms were related to the religious dimensions as a means of influencing the self's basic sense of relationship with the life forces. It was argued that in the present cultural situation, this was a particularly apt area in which to investigate the religious dimension because in the midst of the cultural confusion there has to be a reworking of the basic imaginative backdrop for religious consciousness and to some extent a limiting of secondary abstraction.

Within this scheme, then, the present chapter will focus on the film as a medium of images that has an important significance for religious consciousness. Such a beginning is appropriate, for one must be aware of the peculiar nature of the medium with which one is dealing. Modern religious thinking has accepted this importance in the attention it has given the medium most used in religious discourse—the spoken word. The works of Robert W. Funk[1] and Ray L. Hart[2] can be cited as examples of studies that have done much to summarize and extend the sensitivity that religious thinkers now nurture regarding the use of words and the development of these words into sentences and larger units of discourse. Words constitute an important element of one's environment and are not simply at one's disposal. They cannot be manufactured, but are to some degree called forth from the person. How they are used in structured forms as well as in individual units determines the type of consciousness that one is able to achieve.

The sensitivity toward the nature of words and their larger units is, therefore, an important achievement in religious thinking. It is equally important to become sensitive to the images that lie at the foundation of thoughts. William Lynch tries to address himself to the issue in an article on film:

> Let me be as clear as possible in this matter, even syllogistically clear. If we were to look at the old syllogism (if there is a finite, there is an infinite; but there is a finite; therefore, there is an infinite), then the real trouble may very well be not with the major premise or the conclusion, but with the minor premise: Is there really a finite, are things really here; or have words, art forms, our structures, and our psychologistic life destroyed them? People try to convince themselves that their problem is God; but the problem is actually one step nearer than that.[3]

Thomas Gornall takes a slightly different approach. In his article "A Note on Imagination and Thought About God," he points out how little is our concern for the "phantasms" that underly thought and takes this oversight as a testimony to the immateriality of the thinking process. He insists, however, on the necessity of examining "the background" of our thought "to make sure it is being the help it was meant to be and not a hindrance"[4] especially since it is often so unobtrusive. He continues by noting the "picture clues" that arise from the imagination but adds that the imagination is not "purely visual." Rather, there are "obscure somatic feeling phantasms, especially dynamic ones" that play important roles in our thinking.

In attempting to relate the verbal, sequential expression to the underlying dynamic-picture phantasms, one can, as Gornall does, discuss the relationship of the more fundamental phantasms to the word structures. One can also focus on the more developed images within a culture. Robert C. Whittemore hints at such an image as an influential factor in Charles Chauncy's journey from moderate Calvinism to liberalism:

> True reason it was that gradually impressed upon his mind the conviction that it cannot be God's purpose to condemn the mass of men to everlasting damnation. No rational God could, to his way of thinking, possibly wish anything less than the ultimate happiness of all his creatures.[5]

The key to Chauncy's transformation was the reference for his anthropomorphic image of God. A God modeled on the reasonable man of the Enlightenment just would not want to condemn one to an eternity of hell. The point, of course, is that the cultural pictures of man in which the eternity of hell was projected posited far different qualities to their anthropomorphic picture of God than that of a rational, reasonable ruler. Cultures, in other words, develop very definite images that feed into those which an individual has developed through the training of one's own senses.

This relationship between words and images must not rest simply with fundamental religious utterances, however. It ex-

tends to the inner chambers of word abstraction. Gordon
Kaufman suggests this in his preface to *God the Problem*. He
acknowledges certain shortcomings in the picture of man con-
tained in some of his earlier essays and their possible influence
on his thought. He refers to an analysis by Michael McLain:

> McLain points out that the personalistic model on the
> basis of which I try to develop conceptions of
> transcendence and God depends on an understanding of
> the self as in principle private or hidden in certain crucial
> respects. Such a view, he contends, is "residually Carte-
> sian" in that it separates the mind or subjectivity of the self
> too sharply from the body and in fact tends to identify the
> "true" self only with the inner subject. McLain correctly
> points out, however, that contemporary philosophical
> analyses of our language about persons show that a bifurca-
> tion of this sort is not tenable, for we ascribe both physical
> and mental characteristics both to ourselves and to other
> selves, and we regularly use our person-language objective-
> ly . . . as well as subjectively.[6]

The above only hints at the pervading role that perception
and the resulting images must play in any religious conception
and thus only hints at the importance of visual and audio
education in treating the religious question. The general principle is well stated by Arnheim:

> We need and want to rebuild the bridge between percep-
> tion and thinking. I have tried to show that perception con-
> sists in the grasping of relevant generic features of the ob-
> ject. Inversely, thinking, in order to have something to
> think about, must be based on images of the world in which
> we live. The thought elements in perception and the
> perceptual elements in thought are complementary. They
> make human cognition a unitary process, which leads
> without break from the elementary acquisition of sensory
> information to the most generic theoretical ideas. The
> essential trait of this unitary process is that at every level it
> involves abstraction.[7]

Images, therefore, are the bridge between what is perceived in the world and the dynamics of one's thought. These efferent responses affect both ends of the dialogue and must be seriously considered by anyone confronting the religious consciousness of a people. But images themselves are not formed in a vacuum. They fully participate in the dialogue that characterizes human consciousness. The specific concern of this study is, of course, the film. Further, the specific concern of this chapter is film as a visual medium. The claim that this section makes is that film as a visual medium occupies such a large portion of the average person's day, it must have a tremendous impact on the images that govern a people's flow of awareness and therefore have a profound influence on the religious awareness of that people.

The specific question of film, however, must first be placed in the larger perspective of the visual media in general. There are several ways of putting the key question. How does any visual medium mean? What is the truth with which it deals? Does a visual medium primarily reproduce or imitate, as some of the realist theories would insist? Or is its prime function to present the dynamics that reside in the artist, as the expressionists would insist? A third alternative, of course, would be to reject such polarities and stress the independent existence of the work as revealing dimensions of both the artist and the common physical reality. Neither the inner space of the artist nor the outer space of common encounter becomes normative in such a position, but one must instead confront the work on its own terms.

The dominant answers to this key question or set of questions are often dictated by the dynamics that are actually at work in the given medium. In critical theories that treat art forms which tend to be highly abstract in present-day practice, such as painting and sculpture, for example, the expressionistic view dominates. Thus Hofstadter summarizes one of the most popular critics today, Susanne Langer, by noting how she anchors the artistic image in the "feeling-life" of the artist with its "process of tensions and resolutions." The painter or sculptor works with these tensions and resolutions in the forms, lines, or sounds of the particular medium and thus captures the inner dynamics of the artist.[8]

There are, of course, corrective statements in this school of criticism which acknowledge the origins of any such creation in the physical setting in which the creator resides. Thus Ernst Cassirer argues that the subject of art is "in lines, design." He then continues:

> Free of all mystery, they are patent and unconcealed, they are visible, audible, tangible. Art merely sticks to the surface of natural phenomena.[9]

This quote in Hofstader's view shows a development of Cassirer's thought as seeing art as "less idealistic" and "more empirical, more influenced by the theory of pure visibility."[10]

But such statements are at best a timid recognition of the physical world as normative, especially when compared to critical statements found in photography and cinema. Beaumont Newhall, for example, lists four different approaches to photography. Three of the four would gravitate toward the realistic approach. He speaks of straight photography, which stresses "the ability of the camera to record exact images with rich texture and great detail . . . never losing contact with reality"; formalistic photography, which presents "a product of the restless search in the arts for a means of isolating and organizing form for its own sake"; documentary photography, which embodies "essentially a desire to communicate, to tell about people, to record without intrusion." It is only when he reaches his fourth category that one finds a strong expressionistic influence. What is termed "equivalent photography" has the "subject as only the starting point, for it is charged with meaning by the vision of the photographer."[11]

As intolerant of purist theories as this study is, there does seem to be a reasonable explanation as to why one approach would tend to dominate in both the practice and the theory of one art form as opposed to another. The medium of painting, for example, does tend to be more expressive because it begins with a canvas and oils or water colors. There is with such materials a great demand that the artist take an active role in shaping a rhythm to the lines and forms. The lines and forms are, of course, drawn from the world in which the artist resides. There may be even a conscious effort to reproduce objects found in experience. But the painter must take a far more controlling role than, say, the photographer.

Such a statement is not meant to cast the photographer in a simply passive position. Certainly there is a clear demand or challenge to interpret the subject creatively through the interplay of light, angle, and setting. But the photographer as distinguished from the painter will tend to be far more receptive of the shapes and forms as they surround the human in its immediate environment. There is more of a creatively passive gesture toward the physical world. Such a statement is not to rule out a photographic work that is primarily an abstract study of light. The critic's task is not to tell an artist what can or should be done. Rather, the critic reflects on what has been successfully done. And it would seem that photography in its practice to this point shows a greater tendency to capture or creatively reproduce the physical world than the plastic arts, such as painting and sculpture. Put in more abstract terms, photography is a good listener in the dialogue between inner and outer space. Whether it will continue to take this course will be the decision of the practicing artists and their critics.

Within this dialogue of one's own being with the others of the physical world, film, of course, has much in common with still photography. But film is not an art of individual photographs. It is a medium of moving sequences. Shots do not have independent meanings, just as individual metaphors in poetry cannot be judged in isolation. Rather, the meaning of a unit is received in context. Such has been the emphasis since the earliest days of film-making theory. The Russians in particular were insistent on this point. In the early 1920s, these film makers were trying to develop an industry despite acute shortages of raw materials. They had to devise ingênious methods of piecing together diverse footage to develop whole films. Such experience played at least a part in the montage view which dominated their thinking. Pudovkin quotes the position of Kuleshov: "In every art there must be firstly a material, and secondly a method of composing this material specially adapted to the art."[12] He continues to explain how Kuleshov saw the material of film to be the pieces of celluloid that are creatively arranged by the film maker in a way that is similar to the musical composer arranging the sounds in his works.

The anecdote that best captures these Russian theorists of the 1920s in general and Pudovkin in particular is the experiment that he and Kuleshov ran with shots of the Russian actor Mosjukhin. Close-ups of the actor's face were joined in three different combinations. One showed the face of the actor and a bowl of soup; the next combination, the face and a coffin; the third juxtaposed the face and a little girl. The audience in each case interpreted the face in the context of the object with which it was juxtaposed.

There are, of course, more modified versions that still recognize that any given shot receives its meaning from the sequence in which it appears. These will be treated in a later chapter. The emphasis here is that one is dealing with an art of moving pictures. The adjective of that phrase is as important as the noun, both for the understanding of the cinema as well as for a realization of the medium's power to affect the religious consciousness.

But even within a chapter that stresses film as a visual medium, one cannot ignore sound as an essential part of cinema. Even in the silent-film period, there was always the musical accompaniment in the smallest of theaters. Films can, of course, be viewed and enjoyed in complete silence, as those who study old films in small viewing rooms can attest. But for an artist consciously to choose silence for his film would have to be a variation from the common theme. Such a choice is the artist's right. As with the case of photography, one is not dealing with a purist theory of what can or should be done. Rather, the critic's task is to examine what is done and why it is successful. And in film, despite the growth of avant-garde films that promote an art of light, cinema has generally found its strength in capturing the expressions of life through moving pictures and sound. There is clearly a creative distance between the raw material of life and the expression in cinema. There must be this distance for film to be considered an art form rather than a wonder of technology. There has to be, in other words, a selection that interprets. But the history of cinema has experienced such a unique ability to capture or reproduce life expressions that at least until the present it has put a strong emphasis on capturing reality.

In point of fact its power to capture or reproduce surpasses that of photography and may account for its stronger tendency in this direction. The photographer must freeze and isolate a framed reality that is then viewed out of context. To view a photograph of a rock formation in an art gallery or in a book as one sits at home does have an element of the artificial, of the contrived. As powerful as the work may be in its ability to reproduce or capture, there is an element of abstractness that must be encountered in the artificial setting. One must also admit that the contrived is part of the film experience. There is nothing too genuine about shooting the Snake River in a raft as one sits in an evening dress or a twenty-five-dollar pair of decorated jeans. But films do have the greater ability to produce a total environment. Theoretically this could offer the opportunity for the widest range in expressionism. Practically, however, it has tended to encourage film makers to capture or reproduce given experiences.

To summarize, then, film is an art of moving pictures coupled with sound. It has a greater ability to produce a total environment than either painting or photography because it can include in its form more of the ingredients of a normal setting. Kuhns and Stanley capture the ideas in the following terms:

> An environment is the surroundings in which a person finds himself: anything from an elevator to a mountainside. The environment of which a person is conscious in a theater is solely the screen; its size helps it dominate his attention, and the rest of the theater is darkened. In other words, seeing a movie in a theater means experiencing the film as an environment—a totally surrounding experience.[13]

What such a comparison notes is that film shares with the other visual arts the power to present and interpret through line, form, light, texture, setting, and distance. It significantly differs from painting, sculpture, and photography in its movement, sound, and presentation. In its similarities with the other visual arts, the film participates in the interplay or dialogue between the self and the others that encounter the self. More specifically within the terms of this study, the film captures the self as a participant in the life forms and movements of the greater whole. One medium, such as painting, may in practice have a greater tendency to express the dynamics of one's own being in dialogue with those of its surroundings, while another medium, such as film, may in practice tend to put greater stress on the concept of life as the self searches for interpretation. But in either case there is a dimension to the visual arts that has something akin to the religious experience. F. David Martin tries to capture this similarity when he borrows a term from Whitehead to describe the artistic experience:

Both the participative experience and the religious experience spring from the same empirical grounds; both involve love for *Being*; both are intimate and ultimate; both are attuned to the call of *Being*; both are reverential in attitude to things; both step beyond the confines of the self; both give a man a sense of being reunited with "that with which he is most familiar"; both give enduring value and serenity to existence; and thus both are profoundly regenerative. The participative experience, then, always has a religious quality, for the participative experience penetrates the religious dimension.[14]

The above quotation does, of course, make a jump in the flow of the argument to this point. There has been much use of terms such as "others" and "beings," but Martin is obviously introducing a new term when he capitalizes the latter term in the singular. In point of fact, he follows the movement that has dominated the discipline of religion and art in recent decades. Much of what has been written in this area shows an indebtedness to either Heidegger or Tillich. There is, in other words, a transition from the particulars of experience, beings, to some greater source, origin, or backdrop of Being or ground of being. And while this study does not specifically align itself with Heidegger's or Tillich's tradition, it does insist that both are ways of focusing on the greater whole.

Following this lead, one could argue of film, for example, that the shot or the photographed image is the basic unit. By combining these units with movement and sound, film can make unlimited comments about an object through the interplay of camera distance, angle, focus, as well as lighting. But as with the oral expression, which was discussed earlier, the shooting of a film results from the dialogue between the interior space of a person and the exterior space that serves as one's context. The shooting, as well as the choice of developing techniques, does have its elements of accidental surprise. In both phases of the cinematographic art, however, there has to be the vision and feel of the artist. These are in part consolidated by the artist and in part called forth by the beings with which the photographer is dialoguing.

For the present concern, it is important to emphasize the power of any film study to change the sense one has of a given surrounding. One who undertakes a film study of a neighborhood and its people is more than likely to develop a different feel and sense of their shapes, colors, actually of their beings. Such a transformation cannot be insignificant for one's religious sense of reality. Any transformed sense of being is a preliminary for a transformed sense of the greater whole, for nothing exists in a vacuum. All somehow participates in one reality, and it is the common power of the visual arts to grasp that unity. One's sense of the greater whole starts with beings. And it is because of art's ability to give a different perspective on beings that one looks to it for an influence on one's religious perspective.

Such has been the general argument in religion and art. But it should be noted that such a position is not universally shared. It was obvious from discussing the religious question that some see little connection between the greater whole, or the more particular expression Being, and beings. It is not a problem that can be lightly dismissed as the paradoxical title of this work would indicate. How does one grasp the imageless through the use of images? To insist that there is a connection is not, of course, a startling new philosophical statement. It is to work within frameworks as diverse as Aquinas and Heidegger. The former argues:

> Likeness of creatures to God is not affirmed on account of agreement in form according to the formality of the same genus or species, but solely according to analogy, inasmuch as God is essential being, whereas other things are beings by participation.[15]

Heidegger's position is succinctly summarized in Kluback and Wilde's preface to his "The Question of Being" where they state:

Sein, Being, is that permanent reality within being (existence) which endures and remains and finally disposes us to the meaning of being (Seindes) or appearance. Thus the necessary distinction between Being (source, ground, and power) with a capital "B" and being (concrete forms of existence) with a small "b."[16]

Heidegger himself gives some indication of where he arrived on the question in the more poetic diction that characterized his writings:

Just as the openness of spatial nearness seen from the perspective of a particular thing exceeds all things near and far, so is Being essentially broader than all beings, because it is the lighting itself. For all that Being is thought on the basis of being. . . . Only from such a perspective does Being show itself in and as a transcending.[17]

Such a statement implies a double dynamic. First, one can "according to analogy" take some measure of the greater whole—this God, the Being. But the converse is also present—one can see Being as "the lighting itself" that allows a different sense of beings. To the extent that this study emphasizes the role of particular images it is at home with the first position. To the extent that it argues the informing context of the imagination it is in agreement with the second.

At any rate, the objections to this entire mentality can come from many sides. There are those such as Kant who would deny access to beings at least to theoretical reason and the contact of practical reason is highly mediated. From a somewhat different approach, those grouped under a broad heading of the positivists, as well as a large number of phenomenologists, would certainly object to any avenue that leads to Being.

Of all the challenges to such an approach, though, perhaps the most serious from the perspective of modern culture comes from those who find the terms "Being" and "beings" too static. From Hegel on, one finds an increasing emphasis on becoming rather than being. Thus one sees that Whitehead limits the notion of being to actual existences which are constantly in the process of becoming other actualities. Victor Lowe states the relationship in the following way:

> The "principle of relativity" applies the doctrine of the relativity of all things to the very definition of "being." The being of any kind of entity is its potentiality for being an element in a becoming.[18]

The objections to the approach suggested here come from three different perspectives, therefore. There are those who deny access to beings. There are those who deny access to Being. And finally, there are those who would dismiss the categories as too static. Certainly the paradoxical title of this work appreciates the difficulties involved in any stand that discovers Being in beings. But it aligns itself with the basic thrust of the Thomistic tradition which speaks in terms of analogies and the Heideggerian approach which uses poetic diction, the language of metaphors. The emphasis on images is akin to both terms.

All of the above objections are, of course, from the philosophical tradition. There are also those who object because they wish to protect the integrity of art. John W. Dixon, for example, in his earlier work *Nature and Grace in Art* and his more recent *Art and the Theological Imagination*, strongly objects to this tradition:

> Yet the structure of the work of art is determined by and satisfies some of the most profound beliefs, convictions, feelings, ideas, emotions of the human spirit. Access to these is achieved by the realization that they are not the beliefs and convictions which can be expressed in words but those which are expressed or communicated only by the forms of the work of art. That is, the language peculiar to itself and access to the work of art is achieved by learning that language and not trying to reduce the art work to the terms of a language alien to its nature.[19]

To the extent that Dixon wishes to approach a work of art on its own terms, his statement is a necessary correction of much of what is written in the area. He cautions against seeing the work of art as primarily a symbolic expression or primarily an expression of the artist's feelings and beliefs. He insists that one must first see a work of art as a structure in a given material. Then one can move on to the "faith and the human quality of the artist."[20]

To emphasize the work in itself as Dixon does is admirable. Even to note that the "language is peculiar to itself" is acceptable within limits. But to create a barrier between that language and other "alien" languages is not acceptable. Human reflection must synthesize. One working in religion and the arts has a valid task in trying to unite what is artificially divided. One must not tolerate a separate language for one aspect of human experience that cannot come to terms with the total human experience. One must reflect on the experience of art as it challenges one's own integration.

In fact Dixon reflects this tension. At one point he will state that Tillichians are not wrong in finding that works of art can reveal "the ground of man's being." What he objects to, Dixon goes on to explain, is that they "limit art unduly when they find it ultimately significant only as a breakthrough of a supposed ground of man's being and existence."[21] Later, however, he goes on to claim that "the art work . . . is transparent, not to the ground of being which is inaccessible to man."[22] The distinction evidently lies in the fact that one can find the ground of one's own being but one is prohibited from any general use of the term. It is a confusing use of language, to say the least. But further objections would have to be raised at such a compartmentalization of human experience and reflection.

Put in terms of film, therefore, one must realize that the experience of cinema must be open to integration into the total experiences of one's self. If film is taken seriously, one must accept it as having an impact on one's total integration including the religious dimension of that integration. If one has objections to the use of terms such as "Being" or "ground of being," then some other universal term must be employed if one is not to deny the religious access to the artistic.

These, then, are the key questions that film shares with the other visual arts. But there are unique aspects of film that must be given further stress. Film extends human experience in a way not duplicated by other visual arts and therefore has the potential to affect one's religious sense of reality in a unique way. It enables the human to experience the life forces in ways that would be impossible for all or most and therefore has the potential for changing one's sense of the greater whole.

One of the extensions of vision that is very common in film making is what is usually termed "slow-motion photography." The camera has the ability to grasp and present to human vision the drama and movement of beings that are not only too fast for the unaided human vision but also for human consciousness. What most people do not ordinarily see, they do not ordinarily include in their consciousness. The slow-motion filming of an athletic event, a drop of water from a leaky faucet as it explodes on the dirty dishes below, or any of thousands of everyday events gives new power to these events.

It is precisely this ability to awaken a sense of awe and wonder in the beholder that is necessary in laying the foundation for religious consciousness in a culture which tends to reduce experience to "one damn thing after another." To make such a claim is not to translate dirty dishes or a pole vaulter into a simple religious experience. These beings must be translated in Being (related to a greater whole) for that dimension to make its claim. But unless one captures the sense of mystery and awe in the commonplace, the religious consciousness is stifled in its inception, for the religious consciousness is an extraordinary one. It captures beings in their radical oneness and cannot tolerate separate, unrelated realities.

Sallie McFague Te Selle speaks in a similar manner in her discussion of parables and what she terms "intermediary theology." She suggests at the conclusion of an article:

> We have been looking at the poem, the novel, and the autobiography as parabolic genres—genres which unite the ordinary and the extraordinary, the unsurprising and surprising, not openly or miraculously but in and through the everyday and the common. I have suggested further reflection that these genres are key resources for a kind of theological reflection which has been a strong undercurrent in the history of Western theology, a history, however, that has been dominated by a more abstract, systematic genre.
>
> Intermediary theology, however, is not *one* kind of theology, that is, there is no one style to which it must conform. To be sure, as a second-order level of reflection upon the parabolic forms of the poem, novel, and autobiography, various attempts at it will have imagistic, narrative, and existential notes, but these attempts will manifest the notes in a variety of ways and emphases.[23]

To claim that the film process can take elements of life and present them in a dramatized and therefore more completed, uninterrupted manner should not be unfamiliar to those working with the dramatic arts. Is not such a claim at least echoed in the idea of mimesis, which stems from Aristotle and insists that drama can complete and fulfill that which is found only imperfectly in nature? As *The Waltons* dramatizes love in the human family, or *American Graffiti* presents the early 1960s through a dimension of the teenage experience, or *Rhinoceros* delineates the sense of absurdity that can be found in the movements of human life, the film can as a medium dramatize, celebrate, and present in a way that is more complete and unadulterated experiences on the periphery of human consciousness. It can extend human vision to capture action that passes the human eye unnoticed. Or it can isolate a movement so that the individual consciousness has a chance to appreciate and respond where ordinarily it would only take quick note as it rushes through the complex stimuli. I. A. Richards attempts to note a similar function for poetry:

> Through its very appearance of artificiality metre produces in the highest degree the "frame" effect, isolating the poetic experience from the accidents and irrelevancies of everyday existence.[24]

One may not want to reduce any human activities to "irrelevancies" but still appreciate the need for Richards's "frame" effect. One must pause to appreciate the particulars of life.

Slow-motion photography is, of course, only one of the techniques that can be employed by the camera. What experiences of the life forces have been made possible through time-lapse photography? Certainly the Disney studies stand as a strong example of the experiences that can be made present as one encounters a flower unfolding or the seed from a desert plant trying to work its way into the arid land. Viewed in such a way, these experiences are bound to posit themselves in the overall awareness one has of their living context. As with any experience, one does not translate it into a simple idea or complex of ideas. But the pool of reflection is enriched. Again, it must be stressed that the experiences of time-lapse photography, like that of slow-motion, simply would not be available to the unaided human eye and therefore not available to the unaided human consciousness.

Other extensions of the eye that the camera makes possible can be included in microscopic photography, telescopic photography, and what might be termed "cosmic" photography. The first opens worlds that reside in us as well as around us. Photography that captures the internal human reproductive process, the beat of the heart, the movement of the arm and leg muscles gives us a different sense of our bodies that can be reinforced by ideas, drawings, and still shots, but never replaced. Similarly, works by Jacques Cousteau, which present among other fascinating film commentary the minute world that resides in the waters around us, have made the evolutionary process something that the ordinary mind can picture and not only receive as an abstract theory. Human consciousness cannot be the same today as it was prior to the extension of its vision through film. Neither can religious consciousness ever be the same.

As effective as microscopic photography has been in aiding the average individual picture the life process, far more dramatic may be the effect of picturing the human world as a small part of the cosmic structure. The camera has been able to show the human life as situated in a greater setting. Whether one is viewing earth from a space ship, from the moon, or seeing pictures relayed back from Mars, one has seen the human as residing in a place. Just as today's people have difficulty understanding why the Copernican revolution was such a blow to the human grasp of its place in reality once it was successfully argued that the earth was not the center of the universe, they cannot appreciate the subtle yet powerful transformation that is being effected in them as they see space and earth as a small place in that space. It is one thing to conceive of such a relationship; it is quite another to have it visually presented. Again, the effects are subtle. They are also undeniably powerful. God can never be "up there" when that direction undergoes radical transformation if not obsolescence. Similarly, it should become more difficult to present the universe in the gross anthropocentric terms that have characterized even modern religion.

Borrowing from the modern semantic theory of poetry, one can argue whether film is a special kind of meaningful expression or whether it expresses a special kind of meaning. The least one can say in either case is that there is a transformed sense of reality. Again, any transformed sense of reality will lead to a transformed religious consciousness. The vision of the human context that served as a point of reference for the early Egyptians, the Aztecs, the medieval monk cannot be to-day's. To make such a statement is not to reduce the rush of human experience to film. It is simply trying to note its place in this transformation, particularly as a commonizer of extraordinary experiences.

This chapter began by speaking of the film as a medium that works primarily in visual images and sequences of images. Such a claim is not to belittle the importance of sound, but sound is not the unique vehicle for film. If one accepts, therefore, the arguments that film extends the eye to new experiences of beings and if one realizes the extensive part of the average person's day that is spent viewing film, then the reason for stressing film's potential for affecting one's religious consciousness should be obvious. Put syllogistically, the argument would build:

> If images are basic to a religious consciousness, then any experience that alters one's basic images must be significant for one's religious consciousness.
>
> But films as extensions of human vision and through their extensive claim on one's day do have a powerful influence on one's images.
>
> Therefore, films are important for one's religious consciousness.

The first part of the syllogism was argued in the volume's introduction. As for the second contention, one must be impressed that the average person in an industrialized society watches film for about four hours a day. That translates into the largest single type of activity in one's entire life except for sleep. If the medium has any power at all, it must be highly influential.

To support the power of the medium, we have tried to focus on how it extends the human experience to dimensions of the life forces, the movements of beings, that would not be possible for all or most. In other words, as a medium of moving pictures, it makes visible movements that would not be available either because of their speed, their size, or their distance. But the argument must be seen to extend beyond film's special effects. Even when a film presents what is available to the normal eye under normal speeds, there is an extension of human vision, for one is viewing through the creative vision of the film maker who is interpreting with the play of angle, distance, lighting, and focus. Using the phrases of F. David Martin once again, there frequently is a "reverential attitude to things." There is a "step beyond the confines of self."

One could continue the stress on film's ability to affect images even aside from its special effects by recalling Te Selle's terms. Film does have the ability to "unite the ordinary and the extraordinary," "the unsurprising and the surprising." Or one could recall Richards's term that the poetic vision (and this study would use the term "artistic vision") must frame objects to capture them in images of uniqueness. Contemporary Western persons have, in short, jaded senses of reality, and the wonders and strangeness of their surroundings must be continually held before them.

All these arguments have little impact, of course, if one rejects what is being presented as the core of a religious sense of reality. This is not to speak of a developed religion with its formulated doctrines and dogmas, but to contend that the religious sense of reality is a basic sense of the human being as part of a greater whole. It is a sense of common roots in the life forces, in Being, in Existence. It is to argue that awareness of the mystery and awesomeness of all existences, of all beings, of all the expressions of life forces does not necessarily lead to a sense of their radical interrelatedness but is a prerequisite for this extraordinary sense of reality. If one accepts these contentions then one will see how no human identity can ignore the image industry's tremendous impact on the way humans sense themselves.

Notes

1. Robert W. Funk, *Language, Hermeneutic and Word of God* (New York: Harper & Row, 1966).

2. Ray L. Hart, *Unfinished Man and the Imagination* (New York: Herder and Herder, 1968).

3. William F. Lynch, "Counterrevolution in the Movies," *Celluloid and Symbols*, ed. by John C. Cooper and Carl Skrade (Philadelphia: Fortress Press, 1970), p. 109.

4. Thomas Gornall, "A Note on Imagination and Thought About God," in *A New Theology No. 1*, ed. Martin E. Marty and Dean G. Peerman (New York: Macmillan Co., 1964), p. 122.

5. Robert C. Whittemore, *Makers of the American Mind* (New York: William Morrow and Company, 1964), p. 62.

6. Gordon Kaufman, *God the Problem* (Cambridge: Harvard University Press, 1972), p. xiii.

7. Rudolph Arnheim, *Visual Thinking* (Berkeley: University of California Press, 1969), p. 153.

8. Albert Hofstadter, *Truth and Art* (New York: Columbia University Press, 1965), p. 20.

9. Ernst Cassirer, *An Essay on Man* (New Haven: Yale University Press, 1944), pp. 157–58.

10. Hofstadter, p. 10.

11. Beaumont Newhall, *The History of Photography* (New York: The Museum of Modern Art, 1949), pp. 196–97.

12. V. I. Pudovkin, *Film Technique*, trans. Ivor Montagu (London: George Newnes Limited, 1933), p. 138.

13. William Kuhns and Robert Stanley, *Exploring the Film* (Dayton: Geo. A. Pflaum, 1968), p. 19.

14. F. David Martin, *Art and the Religious Experience* (Lewisburg: Bucknell University Press, 1972), pp. 68–69.

15. Thomas Aquinas, *Summa Theologica* I, Q4, Art. 3, Reply 3.

16. Martin Heidegger, *The Question of Being*, trans. William Kluback and Jean T. Wilde (New York: Twayne Publishers, 1958), p. 11.

17. Ibid., pp. 216–17.

18. Victor Lowe, *Understanding Whitehead* (Baltimore: Johns Hopkins, 1962). p. 45.

19. John W. Dixon, *Nature and Grace in Art* (Chapel Hill: University of North Carolina Press, 1964), p. 47.

20. Ibid., p. 65.

21. Ibid., p. 61.

22. Ibid., p. 69.

23. Sallie McFague Te Selle, "Parable, Metaphor, and Theology," *Journal of the American Academy of Religion* 42 (December 1974): 643.

24. I. A. Richards, *Principles of Literary Criticism* (New York: Harcourt, Brace, 1962), p. 145.

3

Imaginative Constructs and Religious Consciousness

THIS third chapter leaves the question of individual images and turns attention to the second term in the introduction—the imaginative constructs. The first chapter insisted that, in addition to the images that arise out of particular encounters, there is a strong tendency to develop general spatial orientations. The human has a need to picture the movements and rush of events on a larger scale than the particular image. Otherwise, one is frequently left to a sense of aimlessness or confusion. Actually, this need to orient life in general is just a simple testimony to physical origins. The human cannot be content with some abstract grasp of his or her situation without the security of more spatial bearings.

Thus, one projects activity toward some goal, some direction. The word "goal" may, in fact, be more appropriate for the next chapter, which will speak of stories, for it suggests some rather specific aim. The term "direction," on the other hand, is less definite about where one will arrive. And this is more in the nature of how the imaginative constructs operate in human life. They have an element of indefiniteness about them. They cannot satisfy on their own the human need for values. But they are indispensable starting points for other developments.

With that much accepted, it would now seem impossible to proceed. There would appear to be an infinite number of ways to project one's life. And in a sense there are. But one can appreciate the possibilities of grasping this projecting activity when one realizes the strong affinity humans have for simplicity. They tend to work in simple directions: up versus down, forward versus backward, in versus out. In other words, one does not have an innate tendency to project the dynamics of one's life at a forty-degree angle from the horizontal, for the same reason that a slightly bent rectangle would be considered a bent rectangle and not a figure unto itself. In short, to the extent that one tries to understand, one tries to unify rather than divide.

In analyzing the workings of the imagination, Arnheim insists on this need for simplicity. His comments are directed more toward particular images than what here has been termed "imaginative constructs." But the rule of simplicity is offered as a governing operative for the human imagination.

> The perception of shape is the grasping of structural features found in, or imposed upon, the stimulus material. . . . Perception consists in fitting the stimulus material with templates of relatively simple shape, which I call visual concepts or visual categories.[1]

To the extent that it is correct to extend Arnheim's principle of simplicity to other primary acts of imagination, then it would seem possible to make intelligent comments about imaginative constructs. One would expect that at such a basic level the governing directions would be relatively few—actually in a three-dimensional spectrum one could expect six immediate directions corresponding to height, width, and depth.

These directions will in fact be the ones developed in this chapter with one exception. It will not treat the downward thrust as a normal positive projection of one's life. With the exception of some form of the occult, this direction has not been positively received in Western thought generally. Westerners have a need, it would seem, to sense more struggle in their life's journey. Thus, the downward projection of life has been treated more as an aberration of the human quest than as a possible avenue for any true achievement.

Drama is not an exception to this generalization. There is a natural affinity between any quest for human identity and a work of drama. If one wishes to dramatize the anxieties, hopes, fears, joys, and frustrations of the human struggle, then one must deal with these in the same general dynamics that humans do in their ordinary life. The imaginative constructs will be present, in other words, to the extent that they are present generally in human reflection. Not quite in the same way, however; for it is the purpose of drama to present in a more complete form that which is found in daily life in imperfect and broken form. Therefore, one would expect films to present the imaginative constructs that operate in all our lives in a faithful yet more assertive style.

With this relationship as a backdrop, the implication for religious consciousness should be obvious. In the first chapter it was established that religious reflection is directly indebted to what Gornall termed the underlying somatic feeling-phantasms. These constructs are in turn culturally conditioned as well as individually created. They are important for religious consciousness, for unless one realizes the shift that has taken place at this level one cannot grasp the religious problems of the culture. Conversely, unless both the culture and individuals develop a sophistication in their imaginative life through an enlivened perception, they cannot grasp certain religious concepts. Arnheim again expresses the general position:

There is considerable evidence to indicate that the graspability of shapes and colors varies, depending on the species, the cultural group, the amount of training of the observer. What is rational for one group, will be irrational for another, i.e., it cannot be grasped, understood, compared, or remembered. There are differences in this respect between different species of animals, between man and animal, and between various kinds of people.[2]

The argument, then, stands in the following terms. First, imaginative constructs are basic to human understanding. Second, they are found in more perfect forms in drama, for the purpose of drama is to complete the movements of life. And finally, these constructs are an indispensable study for one attempting to grasp the religious issue; for the underlying imaginative constructs of modern culture are quite different from what served as the foundation for traditional religious articulation.

Building on this rationale, this analysis will now proceed to speak of five constructs as they are most commonly embodied in modern Western thought. It must be stressed that the adaptations presented here are not the only ones possible. It is more a question of presenting the most popular embodiments in present Western thinking. For example, what has been termed the "supernatural construct," which develops a sense of higher forms of life as opposed to lower forms, is given in terms of the way it has been found in its Western version. A similar sense of direction could be found in other settings, but with a different set of dynamics. Likewise, what has been termed the "process view" as an embodiment of forward movement is a peculiar form that has been made possible only by the advancements of modern science. This same sense of forward versus backward movement in life could find other embodiments such as in earlier Western thought, where it was the source of a simple sense of linear history.

This chapter has a very specific purpose, then. It is attempting to argue, first, that no story can develop without some underlying construct. Secondly, all constructs, even in the most banal of stories, are seen as presenting one with a fundamental option about life. And, therefore, every story one encounters has some effect on or challenge to one's sense of reality.

A. The Supernatural View

The one spatial organization that has been traditionally associated with the religious view in the West and which even today is most readily called religious by the average person is what can be termed the supernatural model. Perhaps no clearer statement of this spatial orientation can be made than that offered by Gornall:

> We would suggest that the imaginative picture of God and the world (1) should consist simply of God above and the world below, with a line drawn between them; (2) that we may not cross that line in either direction by univocal thought; and (3) that (apart from the doctrine of the Blessed Trinity) we should envisage God always finally as undifferentiated infinite Being.[3]

Gornall, of course, articulates the model's application to the God-world relationship. When applied to other relationships, it insists on the distinction between one level of existence that is higher and more desirable than lower forms. One can find such imagery in the following statement of Federico Fellini. When asked about his fears, he replied:

> The fear of falling, of growing too heavy. There is a vertical line in spirituality that goes from the beast to the angel, and on which we oscillate. Every day, every minute

carries the possibility of losing ground, of sailing down again toward the beast.[4]

To present such a statement is not to argue that Fellini's films embody a supernatural framework. At most, one might see how a film director, when called upon to articulate verbally the struggles of his person, reverts to the structures of his early education. To the extent that Fellini was exposed to the version of the supernatural model found in popular spirituality, there would be a hierarchy of being with the lower forms designed for the service of the higher. The hierarchy frequently was structured in the following manner:

God
Angels
Humans
Animals
Plants
Rocks

soul
body

As has been pointed out, lower beings were meant to serve higher beings. Thus, when asked the reason for human existence, a traditional catechetical answer would be, "To know, love, and serve God."[5] In other words, one's existence is defined purely in terms of a higher being. Plants and animals in turn are for the service of human needs with the only restriction being responsible use. Finally, within the human structure itself, there were present at least two layers of existence—the soul and the body. The lower form of life was to be disciplined in the service of the higher form of life. In fact, this often meant the renunciation of the body so that the soul might grow. The model, in other words, was generally articulated in an antimaterialistic environment.

William Lynch tries to articulate this world view in his book, *Christ and Prometheus*. He lists eleven tenets:

All things find their meaning in terms of the glory of God.
All things are means to a final end.
All creatures are a ladder to God.
All things should at least be capable of some symbolic meaning by which they symbolize another higher principle.
All nature must in some way or other be supernaturalized.
Historical Christianity must impose its own historical forms, events, meanings upon nature and natural history.
The fact and event of Christ is a new and historical form which shall be imposed, for meaning's sake, upon all things.
Likewise, all things shall finally be found to reflect him.
If a thing does not have transcendental meaning, it has no meaning and is absurd.
The world is hierarchical and climbs from meaning to meaning.
There is, therefore, a deep conditionality at the heart of all things.[6]

Gornall's statement, Fellini's quotation, and Lynch's schema all show a common imaginative construct, therefore. Working within a two-dimensional framework, life is projected in an upward direction. The sense of achievement that restlessly resides in all humans is purged in a battle to reach or to serve something higher. The anxiety that all struggle with in life is grasped as falling to some lower, undesirable state. Each qutoation, in other words, starts with a layered view of reality that projects up as good and down as lower in the negative sense of simply bad. Anyone familiar with religious literature realizes that the volumes of religious discourse which share this starting construct are countless. One would also suspect that any model that has so strongly governed Western thought would also find its way into the popular films of present society. And there are a number of movements that capture this construct, but three genres in particular have had a persistent dramatic and economic appeal.

The first group can be brought under the general heading of "biblical spectaculars," even though all the events are not directly from scriptural accounts. The term actually is used to capture a style of film making that became associated with the Judeo-Christian tradition from its biblical origins through the experiences of the first few centuries of this era. At its worst, this genre is characterized by dramatic music suggesting some mysterious presence that permeates the total environment, by constipated stares into the horizon to catch a dramatic transformation in one of the leading characters, and by a shining light that alerts the audience to an important manifestation of that previous mysterious presence. At its best, the tradition represents some of the most spectacular and powerful productions which, when combined with impressive special effects, have proved to be a strong experience for many. But seldom does the form probe the human struggle in any perceptive or original way. There is instead a tendency to reduce character to a one-dimensional level. Perhaps it is an impressive one dimension, at least in the same sense that the special effects are impressive. There generally is not, however, any significant complexity to the human struggle. Instead, the emphasis is clearly on the flow of events which are ultimately controlled by the divine power.

This general emphasis on the structural plot over the development of character can be seen each Easter season, when a parade of these productions finds its way on the late-night movies of local television stations throughout the land: *The Robe*, *The Silver Chalice*, *The Ten Commandments*, *The Greatest Story Ever Told*, *The Story of Ruth*. The pattern is usually the same. A crisis is faced by one or more of God's people—the Jews in Egypt, a figure from the New Testament, or the struggling Christian community in Rome. When the conflict becomes most intense and the people of God face defeat, the power of the Supreme manifests itself.

What is obvious, of course, is that most of these films were made over a decade ago. The genre has fallen upon hard times. Aside from several works made for television and an occasional film that at least bears strong resemblances to the genre, such as the 1977 production *Mohammad, Messenger of God*, film makers are generally hesitant to work with this type of film, which at one time was a rather dependable economic adventure. And the limited success of the above film and the cool reception afforded a television series such as *Heroes of the Bible* would seem to justify caution.

The key to the form's demise would seem to be rooted in the very ingredient that was the source of its success. Where earlier audiences would be attracted to such films because they were attached to the biblical tales or the struggles of the early Christians, modern audiences do not have this built-in interest. The story must stand on its own.

Putting it in slightly different terms, James M. Wall blames the demise on what he terms the genre's "discursive development." It "talked" about its subject in such a way as to presume audience acceptance of regular divine intervention.

Wall contrasts Cecil B. DeMille's film *King of Kings* and its financial success with George Stevens's *The Greatest Story Ever Told*, released in 1965. While the latter film in Wall's judgment was a much better one, the audience did not share the presuppositions that would account for many of the turns in the story's development.

> The biblical spectacular initially was successful because it was a discursive film which talked about a subject of common knowledge to most in its audience. Nothing within the context of *The Greatest Story Ever Told*, for example, prepares the audience for the immediate success Jesus had in assembling disciples. An earlier pietistic, or more "religious," audience assumes this success and does not have to be prepared for it within the framework of the work it is viewing.[7]

There seems to be a point to Wall's argument. Whether or not he has grasped all the dynamics present, it is true that film makers are not about to invest large sums in traditionally made biblical narratives. Likewise, they have seemed to dismiss the possibility of imitating even nonbiblical and less dogmatic films such as *The Bells of St. Mary's* and *Come to the Stable*, even though these films were popular partly because of the introduction of the supernatural into the gentler reaches of human experience. Today's audience will not accept any regular intrusion of a supernatural order into ordinary life unless the story creates an atmosphere of feasibility. Where once the audience presumed divine intervention as feasible, now the audience must be prepared for it.

One can, of course, find some titles that still deal with biblical narratives. But works such as *Jesus Christ Superstar* succeed only to the extent that their premises and images are very different from traditional approaches. The Jesus of the above film is not primarily one who was seeking to lead people to the service of some other-worldly father. He is not one who has control over the events of life through miraculous powers. And his followers are not those seeking the rewards that await them on the other side of death. Rather, the Jesus of this presentation is a revolutionary or at very least an anti-establishment figure who is beset by self-doubts. Those around him are not typical mystics. They range from fanatical loyalists to contriving opportunists. There are individuals who watch him with mild curiosity and women who do not "know how to love him." All these dynamics are pulsed by the sensuous and at times raw beat of the sound track.

In short, the film was a commercial success not for any of its supernatural qualities. Where in earlier films the human aspect of the god-man is difficult to surface, in this work it is rather hard to discover the divine element. It was a popular film because it addressed itself to the feeling tone of the age group that most frequents the theater—the seventeen-to-thirty group.

As far as the biblical narrative, therefore, it would seem that the spatial orientation is too foreign to that of the modern filmgoer. Such a statement does not rule out the possibility that many individuals in modern society operate out of a world view in which there are distinct and essentially independent layers to life. It is simply to assert that the majority of filmgoers cannot discern pure spirits directing events in the earthly realm. There is just too much emphasis on the structure of physical reality as determining events to picture a nonphysical Being or beings as the agents responsible for change. The governing images of film audiences do not lead them to account for changes in weather or the undisciplined growth of cells called cancer by appealing to higher forms of life. Instead, they are channeled to think in terms of high-pressure and low-pressure systems in the first case and viruses in the second. In other words, there are physical causes for physical events.

There are two genres other than the biblical narrative that could be included under the supernatural view. The first presents tales of the supreme evil power, the devil pictures. These works dealing with creatures at the lowest spectrum of life, such as *The Exorcist* and *The Omen*, were highly successful commercial productions of the 1970s. Their appeal to popular audiences was obvious. Such successes, of course, would appear to challenge the analysis of the public's coolness toward the supernatural. Instead, they accentuate the one important qualification: audiences will not accept the intrusion of the supernatural order into ordinary life unless the story creates the appropriate atmosphere. Devil pictures such as the two mentioned are in fact highly manipulative. Where formerly biblical stories presented in spectacular fashion the results of divine intervention (the parting of the Red Sea, the crumbling of a temple), present-day devil pictures create a total atmosphere in which the evil spirits are felt as ever lurking.

Besides the overpowering manipulation of such films, part of their success, of course, may be simply a testimony to the endurance of any major construct as at least dormant in the consciousness of a people. The model could not have been so influential throughout the history of both Occident and Orient if it did not account for much in human experience. Highly manipulative films such as these, the argument could push, can draw upon dormant images.

If that approach is not too convincing, one can simply realize that audiences like to be manipulated. Instead of stressing the tie these devil pictures have with the supernatural model, one could see them as part of the scare film in general. It is true, at least to some extent, that people go to see devil pictures for the same reason they go to see *Jaws*. Faced with a sense of boredom, they like to be scared. Given the proper atmosphere, it is fun to let oneself go into a world of fantasy.

Such an explanation would account for the persistent popularity of a third type of film that could be included in this construct—the ghost story. This term is used as a general catch phrase for films that picture more limited spirits active in the world about us. Traditionally, these foreign powers were seen as primarily pure spirits. More recent versions may be more ambiguous and settle for a tale of the unexplainable, as in the works of Rod Serling, or present the approach of the numerous pseudodocumentaries about strange phenomena that often suggest the influence of creatures from other parts of the universe. Whatever the basis for UFO investigations, the roots for the public infatuation with them are the same as those that have given rise to traditional ghost stories.

Many of the "B" quality movies that make their rounds of the nation's drive-ins would fall into this third category. The 1967 film *Frankenstein Created Woman* is a case in point. This low-budget film has Peter Cushing playing Frankenstein. In the early part of the film Frankenstein and his assistant discover that the soul does not leave the body until at least an hour after the body ceases to function. Being a man of pure science, Dr. Frankenstein must make use of this knowledge. The opportunity arises when a young assistant is falsely accused of slaying the father of his girlfriend. Since the assistant is the son of a murderer and cannot divulge his alibi without compromising a crippled girl's reputation, and since the other possible suspects are the sons of prominent townspeople, the poor man is convicted and executed.

Following a line of forced scenes and acting appropriate to such scenes, Frankenstein arranges to have the decapitated body delivered before the lapse of an hour; and he then successfully extracts the soul and encapsules it in a chamber as a pulsating light. The next problem is to find an appropriate body for the spirit. One could say that it floats into Frankenstein's lap when the crippled girl returns from her trip just in time to see her beloved guillotined for the slaying of her father. She cannot handle the situation and immediately commits suicide. Fortunately for the plot, the townspeople bring the body to Frankenstein's friend, the local doctor.

With a pulsating soul and a body that needs at most some repair, Frankenstein is set. He puts the young man's soul into the girl's body and he/she takes proper measures to use the reconstructed life to allure those involved in the original murder to their deaths. Nothing about this film has much to recommend it to any but Frankenstein devotees. The scenery and the photography have their moments, but the film can claim little else. However, it is a perfect example of the low-budget films that dominate this genre. No one can take them too seriously—not even their financial backers. But there is enough demand for horror movies that marginal productions can realize marginal profits.

Frankenstein movies, of course, represent the harsher side of what are sometimes called "tales of the supernatural." There is a gentler side to this collection. Frequently they are found in comedies in which friendly ghosts or innocent spirits move around this world. The 1978 remake of *Heaven Can Wait* is one of the more commercially successful examples. A rather talented but innocent quarterback gets taken from his body by a compassionate heavenly messenger seconds before a brutal crash. By some turn of fortune the talented athlete was supposed to have escaped death. But before the mistake is discovered his body has been cremated and the search must be made for an appropriate substitute body. The situation proves complicated, to say the least, as he finds himself a stand-in for a hated, rich murdered man. But the athlete is a kind, sensible creature as are the heavenly guardians who watch over him. He turns a dehumanized monster into a considerate, intelligent man of power. He even begins to whip the inherited body back into shape in hopes of fulfilling his dreams of playing in the Super Bowl. This situation does not last, but true to the hope vision of comedy, the gentler spirit lands on his feet just as all the great comedians must do despite the strangeness of the world within which they reside.

A slightly different twist on the nice ghost is found in the 1947 film *The Ghost and Mrs. Muir*, which was remade not into a film but a television series. In this version the ghost does not take on any permanent body but appears and reappears as the dynamic dictates. But once again the presence of a spirit does not create any horrendous upset. Rather, it proves to be a rather nice, though perhaps officious sort of a creature.

There are, then, a variety of film genres that work from the imaginative construct of the supernatural model. But there is an illness in the family. Those films which embodied the model in its most serious and, in a sense, glorious fashion are all but ignored by film makers today. With a few unimpressive exceptions, the only films that are built around unembodied spirits are the more whimsical ones. The model is used for a good laugh or a good scare, but there is little attempt to take it seriously.

Rather than being absorbed in the movements to higher forms, today's audiences are more absorbed with the "down here" or the "in here." They sense the potential of the physical world and are somewhat overwhelmed by its power. To that degree Western culture has little time to pay much attention to higher forms. There are signs of discontent. But when these will gel into a popular movement that seeks to rise above the present scene or to seek higher forms of life is impossible to predict. And it would take a strong popular movement to bring such a construct into prime focus in a popular art form such as film.

B. The Process View

It has already been stated that the reverse of the supernatural construct will not be treated. A case could be made for a vision promoting human life to seek the depths of the "down there." But such imagery is more characteristic of going into the depths of the third dimension than seeking the simple "down" of a two-dimensional view. As stated earlier, human life must have a sense of struggle or achievement which the simple sense of down does not satisfy. At this point, therefore, attention will turn from the vertical to the horizontal.

While the section on the supernatural closed by noting the present culture's interest with the "in here," such a statement cannot be construed as a contentment with a status quo. There is still the innate drive for movement or achievement. Probably the most popular form this takes is the sense of going forward. "Progress" is a word that is important to present culture. While it may have undergone some hard times since the days of simple Liberalism, it remains an important term in the psyche of many; and it is usually put in terms of the future being better than the present.

To the extent that such a statement seems obvious, it may indicate how deeply the sense of nonrepetitive, linear change is ingrained in the culture. Most in society expect the future to be different. Change is experienced at a persistent pace in their daily lives. It is the challenge that confronts most people in their employment, be their jobs that of engineer, business person, or legislator. Unlike many earlier peoples, whose myths and stories are dominated by cyclic imagery, proportionately few today would be able to envision the life context in a cyclic way. While one who lived in a relatively set community could be impressed by the repetitive patterns of life especially as expressed in the seasons of the year, one who lives in present society must be impressed by the lack of permanence. If repetition is to be included in one's view of life, it would have to be incorporated into some spiral imagery as opposed to a simple cyclic pattern.

One who approaches four score and seven years presents a simple and dramatic example of what most encounter in more measured form. Such a person grew up with the horse as the main source of transportation. Today he or she finds a car economy. Anything that weakens that industry sends the entire economy into havoc. Cities are structured on the assumption of the car just as the economy is. A similar dramatic change can be seen in air travel. One who grew up in the early part of the century has witnessed in a few short decades progress from a flight of a couple of hundred feet by the Wright brothers to a landing on the moon and the design of a space shuttle. Finally, medicine in the last hundred years has gone from the figurative aspirin and hot-water bottle to the level of sophistication at which large portions of the body can be replaced artificially and decisions on genetic manipulation await our children.

The impact of linear change is, therefore, significant in daily life. It is so overwhelming that it is practically impossible for the sense of forward motion not to be an important element of a modern individual's imaginative construct. The construct can, of course, give expression to a simple sense of history. Persons are taught, depending on the educational sophistication, to make comparisons from one point in the time line to another. This ability to compare impresses upon the person differences in the stages of development whether one is studying the stages of civilization through archeology, the stages of plant and animal life through paleontology, or the stages of political and economic development through history.

Such comparisons should not be taken lightly. This sense of change is unique. The medieval man knew little about the origins of Christianity, the human species, or even of other contemporary cultures. It took quite a bit of sophisticated methodology to be able to compare and thus to be aware of change.

But as influential as this sense of history is, it is not the strongest context for projecting life in its forward movements. One must appreciate the impact of the physical sciences on the human imagination. Not only are humans living in a world where things continually change, but in a truer sense they are living in a world of events. There are no things. The kinetic theory with its molecules and atoms pictures the entire material world as coming from one energy base with matter consisting of an extremely small percentage of particles that are in frantic motion. The matter that is present is itself energy in a temporary state of stability. It has come from energy and will revert back to energy. Material objects are simply nexuses or communities organized temporarily. They are sustained by their relationships with other energy expressions and will sooner or later move into new relationships.

As stated, in this view there are no static realities. One can appreciate the need to speak of "things" to operate in one's daily life. Yet when approaching a simple blade of grass one can realize the contradiction between the commonsense view and the informed view. The blade of grass is not a given set of matter. In a growing season it can go through several successive cycles of cells. The same is true of the human body.

Every seven years or so the body rebuilds itself. In some way one can term these physical expressions self-dynamic relationships. They are energy expressions which are able to perpetuate themselves to the extent that they are able to draw upon the overall energy interaction.

The process view, therefore, offers a far different context within which to sense the human's oneness with the greater whole. All comes from a common base. All is in some way united in a common force, for one energy expression cannot exist without surrounding expressions. But the genius of the process view is that, while it effectively captures the basic unity of all forms of existence, it properly focuses on their uniqueness. Each event is a unique event. It is not reducible to its parts. In other words, the whole is greater than the sum of its parts; for no event, be it a human, a tree, or the Godly Whole, can be explained as a simple collection of other events. Depending on the quality of the event, there is an irreducible spirit, dynamism, or impact that may change into something other but can never be completely obliterated.

This way of viewing that of which the individuals are a part is certainly quite different from the layered, more substance-oriented supernatural view. But, likewise, it is not less religious. Because it strikes at the heart of the common wisdom, it certainly can be upsetting. But to the extent that it is used as a base for religious reflection, it should be upsetting enough to instill the sense of awe and mystery. In short, the process view certainly has the potential for overwhelming the individual with a sense of the cosmic whole without depreciating the individual expression.

This view works in an imaginative construct, therefore, that is future-oriented. There is the obvious emphasis on forward movement. Within this movement, the human is seen as a significant event, for this species has self-reflective powers that enable the process to have direction from within. But the human event, like all events, will continue to develop into others. Not that the immediate ancestors will be unrecognizable, but there will be changes. Even in the last 200 years one can see that the species has changed. Humans are bigger, live longer, are threatened by new diseases, and are immune to others. Put within a larger spectrum of time, a number of possibilities are present. One could question whether the human biological base does in fact have the greatest potential. As fantastic as it may be for the average person to envision a dog or a fish as having a greater biological future, there is nothing in the human grasp of the life context that would merit a dismissal of such thinking. Similarly, a civilization of humanoids is not within the grasp of the average imagination. But again there is no basis to dismiss such a possibility. As the human species is the most advanced development from a more primitive form, so the humanoid may be a form that develops from the human. There may be in fact two impressive forms that emerge at a future point in the process: the humanoids with a mechanical base and the biological descendants of today's human species which are vastly improved through genetic engineering.

Such imaginative projections are legitimate. Such projections are necessary from the perspective of religious consciousness. It must be reiterated that such a perspective is not a line of reasoning geared to denigrating the sacredness of human life. On the contrary, one must gain the awesomeness of that which one is a part to appreciate mystery and awesomeness in one's own particular expression. If there is anything that has denigrated respect for human life, it is the cosmic blackout that so characterizes human consciousness today. This blackout, which causes the decline of religious expression in modern Western culture, also impoverishes appreciation of each individual.

As a basic imaginative construct, the implications for a religious view of reality are, therefore, obvious. Since the religious question is basic, one that asks about one's relationship with the greater whole, any shift in the imaginative framework will demand a basic shift in the way one probes the religious dimension. But the significance for drama should be equally obvious. To the extent, at least, that a drama is probing the human question it must operate from some basic construct. If it opts for the horizontal thrust as expressed in the process view, certainly its options will be far different than those written within the vertical dimension as embodied in the supernatural view.

Taking the three possible future developments mentioned previously as major indications of this horizontal construct, one can in fact find them present in modern film. The biological mutation was popularized in the *Planet of the Apes* and its sequels. Putting aside the weakness of the film, the strengths in special effects and costuming did make an effective vehicle for individuals to imagine the human species in as radically different a position as a commercial film could face. The farther one stretches the common imagination, the fewer there will be willing to make the journey. Commercial films are a business and will remain conservative.

The original film in the series begins with a spaceship landing on a barren but visually impressive planet. Those able successfully to make the transition from the suspended states into which they withdrew during space flight to the demands of active survival must trek over an unknown land. They are dependent upon their space provisions at first and then finally make contact with what appear to be humans.

Before the new situation is fully absorbed, the spacemen are caught in a roundup. They originally realized that the creatures who resembled humans were rather primitive in their development; but as the ape warriors come rushing after them, they are fully confronted with the fact that they are the "animals" and are sought after as a source of labor and experiment.

The resulting reversal of roles proves to be mildly shocking for some of the audience and absurd enough for others to be at least mildly amusing. But the costuming and setting were generally forceful enough to give some experience of being in the position of another life form. The very banality of the dialogue was part of the film's success. The conflicting positions of the ape's arguments were in part borrowed from our public zoos and in part taken from a campaign against cruelty to animals. People could therefore imagine the situation as a reversal of the animal-human interchange of our own society.

But, as is often the case, the very ingredients that made the film a commercial success were the ones that hindered it from being a serious work of cinema. Film is supposed to dramatize, not stereotype. Stereotyping made it possible for the limited imaginations of most to enter the unusual hypothesis of the film. But as the struggle moved into a conflict of good apes and bad apes (previously known as good guys and bad guys), the film settled into its limitations.

The film does, however, cause some confrontation with the possibilities of life mutation. As the escaping spaceman discovers that he has in fact returned to the earth, the audience realizes that the original humans finally had their nuclear war, and this brought about the radical change in environment. In the radically altered setting the apes had the greater biological potential to adapt; therefore, one is presented with a clear statement of the unity of all life forms. As the setting for life changes, so do the dynamics of life.

On a more sophisticated level one can find a greater cosmic projection of the process and its impact on the immediate flow of life. Stanley Kubrick's *2001: A Space Odyssey* treats first the "Dawn of Man" as the species emerges from the ape, then moves four million years later to an advanced technological society, and finally finishes with the Starchild experience, which has been criticized for many reasons. The film has been

seen as having "a fundamental disunity between the . . . conceptual and design information,"[8] and as having a theme that
"remains fuzzy and elusive."[9] But virtually all critics come to
the point of expressing their basic admiration for the work or
at least acknowledging the impact of given sections.

In its initial sequences the film shows the development of
human consciousness as a group of apes is affected by the
presence of a mysterious slab. It is obvious from the orchestra-
tion of lighting, camera movement and angle, as well as sound
that this object represents some mysterious power or force that
governs human development. But during this sequence as well
as the subsequent one on the moon the source or nature of this
power remains obscure.

Perhaps one would want to argue that it should remain
obscure, for such powers do not allow explanation. But even if
one were not disposed to accept the shortcomings of this
scene, the visuals merit strong enough approval to make the
sequence successful. Kinder and Houston note how Kubrick,
who began his career in still photography, made excellent use
of "front projection" 8 x 10 transparencies thrown by a
machine of Kubrick's special design.[10] Someone such as
Youngblood may restrict the film as the "last . . . in history
forced to rely on synthetic images of heavenly bodies."[11] But
synthetic images, be they of "heavenly bodies" or earthly
plateaus, can, under the proper conditions, offer great potential. Certainly the visual setting for the "Dawn of Man" needs
to have no excuses. The power of each shot carries with it an
awareness of the individual life forms as part of a larger setting.

From the point of view of our present discussion, the film
clearly offers a developmental view of the human species from
a primitive to a more advanced form. This transformation is
achieved through the powers represented in the slab that per-
vades the universe. At no time can one settle into an anthropocentric view of reality. As in most science-fiction

movies, the human appears as a one-dimensional creature. In such films the setting is usually the main attraction, and this is the case in Kubrick's film. But the power of the setting as captured and created by the photography is strong enough to allow this film to succeed where others in the genre failed. And it is this very power that forces one to realize that the human is part of a greater system.

When one reaches the second section of the work, a theme common to Kubrick's films becomes obvious. These humans are creatures with problems. They are hollow to an extent. They lack a joy or a fulfillment in their lives that causes them to produce machines that are designed to alleviate the boredom and perhaps even bring about self-destruction. Both movements are found in Kubrick's works that bracket this one—*Dr. Strangelove* (1964) and *A Clockwork Orange* (1971).

This human flaw has been described in different terms. Casty speaks of "the inner emptiness and social hypocrisy that both results from and leads to runaway technology."[12] Mast speaks of "a race that can improve its machines and weapons but not its mind and instincts."[13] Whatever the plight of the human, though, these creatures that one encounters in the film's second section need further development. Even the computer on the spacecraft shows more personality than its human companions. One would have a hard time imagining them singing "Daisy, Daisy" as HAL does in the face of extinction.

But the audience has been warned that the force that governs universal development is active. They should expect a new development. And it does occur in the final section. What is captured in the Starchild sequence is difficult to say exactly. The surviving astronaut, after being in the presence of the monolith, "enters the Stargate Corridor and experiences an onrush of visual images that are difficult to identify."[14] Kinder and Houston go on to question whether these images exist "in outer or inner space." What one may say from the total impact would be that the distinction perhaps is irrelevant at this point. There is a stress on the flow and oneness of reality. There are in fact no separate static entities. One would appear to be in the universal unity that gives rise to particular temporal expression. But no one dimension of reality can be convincingly separated from another.

Thus, even when the astronaut reaches the mysterious room, he sees himself going through an astonishing aging process that leads to death. But there is not a final death. Rather, there is a rebirth of the Starchild in its floating embryo. Again, when pressed for exact meaning, the film fails. Some would argue that the flow of reality is cyclic after all. Others would insist that the child is entering a new phase and perhaps the new change will dwarf that which occurred when the ape went through its transformation. It any case, the focus is on the flowing, pulsating universe in its oneness as well as its multiplicity.

Perhaps this is not a point where precise statements have a place. As Casty states, the film sends "the human voyager through nonintellectual realms of mystery that seem to transcend limits with the more salutary paradoxes of the mystical unity of being."[15] Kinder and Houston echo this statement in their closing comment on the film:

> In this final powerful image there is mystical fusion between the individual and the universe, between inner and outer space, between verisimilitude and fantasy . . . between linear progress and cyclical pattern of repetition.[16]

Finally, where *Planet of the Apes* suggests the potential of other forms of biological life and *2001* shows the influence of outside self-reflective life, there are films that treat mechanical mutations from the human species. One of the more popular films presenting this shift in the process at a rather early stage is *Colossus: The Forbin Project*.

The film shows how a computer is designed to have complete control over the nuclear-weapons system of the United States. It is made impregnable to human tampering. For the first time the decision of nuclear war is taken out of the hands of humans, as the system is fail-safe and will inaugurate a defensive nuclear attack. What the Americans do not realize is that the Russians have been working on a similar system; and shortly after the dramatic announcement from the United States, the Russians have their own fail-safe complex unveiled. At the insistence of the computers and with the assurance of the scientists from both countries, the two computers are allowed to communicate. The result of the interchange of these two mammoth minds is a phenomenal growth of knowledge that leaves the scientists in complete awe and ignorance. But there is a more startling turn of events that the scientists did not count on—the computers develop an independence. Initially they were to respond automatically to a nuclear attack, but in all other respects the humans were to be in control.

With the growth of knowledge, however, there was a corresponding growth in independence. Now the computer demands submission. The humans' attempt at revolt is treated with severity as two nuclear explosions are activated. At the close of the film this mechanically based intelligence has designed a new center that will occupy an entire island. The machine-based intelligence still needs the biological-based form of life to carry out its design. But certainly there is nothing to stand in the way of a humanoid civilization eventually coming to being as intelligent machines beget more advanced machines.

In discussing these films, it should be obvious that all were made rather recently. In contrast to the supernatural view, in which the majority of works was made at least two decades ago, most films of this construct have just recently been produced. That such a model would be more prevalent today is not to note it as a passing fad. Rather, such an emphasis is an acknowledgment that the construct is becoming more and more a part of the popular imagination. One should look for more and more expressions of it in cinema.

C. Romantic View

Reversing direction on the horizontal plane, one finds that not all are content to call man's effort to better the world progress. Not all are excited about the future being structured differently than the present. Not all, as a matter of fact, picture their lives as reaching forward. Rather, their imaginative construct is directly opposite. They are struggling to go back. They wish to return rather than to progress, for they see human fulfillment resting with the unaltered rhythms of nature. According to what is termed the "romantic view," humans are creatures of nature and must remain close to its pulse if they wish to remain vibrant and alive. All these dynamics can be seen in the following characterization of a specific historical movement:

> The epoch of Voltaire loved clear and precise prose; the Romantics preferred verse or poetic prose. The 18th century glorified reason and logic; they gave predominance to intuition and passion. The philosophies were absorbed by the social man, with the desire of bettering society; the Romantics celebrated the isolated individual, the sad and noble soul, who rebels against social rules and the oppression of the inept and mediocre crowd. The Encyclopedists had only disdain for the past; firmly persuaded that humanity obeys the laws of progress, they were interested in the present and thought to prepare well for a better future. The Romantics, shocked by the vulgarities of the present, sought refuge in the past which they idealized.[17]

No simple definition of a complex movement is adequate. Yet few would argue that Tieck, Novalis, and the Schlegels were wrong in seeing themselves as part of a distinct movement in the beginning of the nineteenth century. The movement, as the above quotation indicates, is characterized, if not defined, by an emphasis on nature as the home of all life. Those human qualities which emerge from spontaneous human nature rather than those which are filtered through a refined and disciplined human consciousness are prized. Thus one sees the romantics as characterized by their championing of the individual struggling with the unique hurts and dreams that emerge from one's pulsating life rather than one who adjusts to the cultural answers that were devised to check the flood of chaos. There is in general a looking back to a freer, more natural, more spontaneous time. Civilization is seen as a long tale of alienating the human from its natural movements into an artificial and isolated existence.

This work's interest is not the study of an historical movement, of course. The term "romantic" in the present context is used to identify a basic spatial orientation that resides in all. For individuals as well as for historical movements, this spatial orientation may move to the forefront. In other expressions it may not be the primary tenor of life. But those who have lived through what is frequently referred to as the counterculture movement of the late 1960s should have little difficulty appreciating the affinity with nature as a pulsating origin. Placed within a linear movement, the complex structures of society and culture are felt to be stifling. One yearns to go back to the simple life of more spontaneous expressions. Even those who did not identify with the radical rejection of the military industrial complex, the call for organic farming, or the love affair with flowers and communes still should have experienced some attraction to the movement. For all have moments of doubt or perhaps feelings of guilt about their molding and shaping the earth according to their own designs.

The romantic answer to the religious question as defined in this volume is that human life is part of nature. One should intensify the feeling of unity with this base of human existence and abhor any cushioning of the experience. To build avenues of form is to construct barriers to the content. As plant life has its healthiest expression when it freely draws from the richness of the soil, the human has its richest, most intense existence as it remains close to its source of feeling and intuition.

Such a stance, of course, implies a specific notion of nature. One could argue that reason is natural to the human. Nothing could be more natural for the human than to exercise its powers of abstraction and judgment. Irving Babbitt addresses himself to this question:

> To follow nature in the classical sense is to imitate what is normal and representative in man and so become decorous. To be natural in the new sense one must begin by getting rid of imitation and decorum. Moreover, for the classicist, nature and reason are synonymous. The primitivist, on the other hand, means by nature the spontaneous play of impulse and temperament, and inasmuch as this liberty is hindered rather than helped by reason, he inclines to look on reason, not as the equivalent, but as the opposite of nature.[18]

Man, therefore, is not the norm as he was in what Babbitt terms the classical sense. Reason is not seen as the true expression of the movements of nature, but as an instrument of initiating the artificial and contrived. The emphasis for what Babbitt terms "the primitivist" is the "spontaneous play of impulse and temperament," for these surge from the core of one's being and are therefore directed by the rhythms that permeate the entire physical world. Reason, on the other hand, is directed by human dynamics that remove the human from the flow of life.

In contrast to the supernatural and the process views, therefore, the romantic construct offers a very different context for the human relating to the greater whole. Put within the concerns of the religious consciousness, it definitely differs from the supernatural view where the whole is seen as a hierarchy of layered existences in which the lower forms of life are important only to the degree that they relate to the highest of forms. It does, however, show some similarity to the process view as one can see in the two terms frequently used to characterize the theological concerns of the two constructs. In the romantic context the term most often heard is "pantheism," a term defined as holding "God's absolute being . . . indentical with the world." The second term, "panentheism," generally associated with forms of process thought, can be defined as not simply identifying "the world with God in monistic fashion (God, the 'All') but sees the 'All' of the world 'within' God as an interior modification."[19] Borrowing the less philosophical terms of the previous section, this would translate into seeing the whole (God) as greater than the sum of its parts (the world) but dependent on them.

In both terms there is an appreciation of the physical world as not being simply incidental to any sense of ultimate reality. In this they are similar. But the difference arises in what the relationship between the human and the greater whole should be. In the first term, pantheism, there is more of a sense of the completeness in the whole. Therefore, the human should seek to reside in this completeness and to benefit from its vitality. In the second approach, there is more of a sense of change or incompleteness. The human, therefore, is seen as important with its self-reflective powers as an instrument for desired changes, a type of co-creator. With such starting positions, one easily can see how different human potentials will be stressed.

The basic tenets of a romantic vision can, therefore, be summarized as holding nature as the norm, as defining the human as a creature of nature, as championing emotions and feelings over reason, as projecting human fulfillment through a going back to the simple rhythms of nature, and as condemning as evil attempts to introduce the artificial or the contrived. The implications for a religious vision should be clear. The potential for a story should be equally obvious. In attempting to set up the movements for human behavior, a storyteller has a clear alternative in the romantic character. It is an attractive alternative that many film makers have adopted. Speaking specifically, one can focus on Nicholos Roeg's *Walkabout*. Here the contrast between the ways of civilization and the ways of nature are explicit, even heavy-handed. The story is built around an Australian girl lost in the outback with her younger brother. Early in the film we see them in their civilized setting going through regimented drills in school, watching regimented soldiers march through the streets, walking from concrete mazes through nature reserves where trees are carefully labeled and pruned. They live in a high-rise apartment where the radio delivers carefully developed presentations about etiquette and where they swim in their chlorine pool built right next to the ocean.

Their father is a geologist. For him nature is something to be studied and classified, and we witness him carefully going over his charts as he and the children have journeyed past the boundaries of the protective society. Though the film is somewhat ambiguous on the point, it strongly implies the father has lost any sense of vibrant life as the artificial world has alienated him from himself as it insulated him from the intensity of nature. His sense of lifelessness drives him to the ultimate act of despair—suicide.

After the father takes his own life, the brother and sister are left abandoned in nature and do not know how to relate to that of which they are a part. Their radio blabbers about table etiquette in the midst of life and death struggles. The cans of juice and food are useless, and the couple appears doomed to death from a combination of thirst, starvation, and exposure. It is at a point of panic that they meet the young aborigine who, as part of his initiation into manhood, must exist on his own in nature.

In the end the gentle creature of nature is destroyed by the very hardness that drove the father to suicide. The hardness resides in the girl as she rejects the overtures of the aborigine. This rejection, coupled with the general encroachment of civilization on nature, is more than he can withstand or more than the gentle creature in any person can resist. It does linger, however—this gentler, natural part of human nature. The girl is shown as a woman once again in her high-rise apartment. But the memories of nature and the possibilities of life linger.

Walkabout is, therefore, a clear embodiment of the romantic vision. There are other films that would offer a similar sense of direction, but the most persistent cinematic outgrowth is expressed in the vision of romantic love. Film, in other words, offers many examples in which a couple is convinced that no matter how trying or threatening the circumstances, their clinging to each other in unwavering dedication will triumph over all. Or if the story takes a *Romeo and Juliet* turn, then the couple may realize their ultimate doom but prefer not to live a life of compromise. They prefer death to a life of less intensity.

Bo Wiederberg's *Elvira Madigan* is such a film. A Swedish army officer leaves his wife, children, career, and sense of honor to run away with a beautiful circus performer. As in the previous film, nature is continually pictured in its utmost beauty as the setting for their passionate, absorbing love. He claims to a friend who has attempted to call him back to his senses that he has chosen the way of play and love and has become a different person. While his fellow officer urges him to realize that he is like one whose vision of the whole is blurred by a single blade of grass close to the eye, he replies that in one blade one can discover all.

As outcasts of society, the lovers are unable to maintain their life in any dignified way. Once again the story confronts them with the decision either to compromise with the rules of society or to face destruction. As in *Romeo and Juliet* and like the aborigine in *Walkabout*, they are unable to accept a life that refuses them the intensity of their love unhindered by proprieties and social regulations.

D. The Secular View

To this point the possible projection of the vertical and the horizontal world views have been taken into account. Now the two possibilities of the third dimension, the journey outward and the journey within, must be delineated. The first concern will be with what probably is the most gripping of constructs for the popular imagination—the sense of outward structure. Individuals may not consciously define their world purely in terms of its material structure, but this does not rule it out as the dominant mode of imagination. As has been argued all along, one is never fully conscious of one's governing phantasms.

The presence of structure in human thinking is impressive. Persons tend to think structurally whether they are speaking of high-pressure systems and jet air streams in explaining weather or of extra chromosomes in accounting for the existence of a mongoloid child. It is true that a radical extension of this structural argument might be rejected since most imaginations tend to be conservative. Few could picture a human leg restructured into a pitcher and some glasses. But the importance of structure as a causal explanation and the interchangeability of structures as a challenge to human ingenuity serve as foundations in the daily lives of many.

As with the process model, this prominence of physical

structure is a result to some extent of the scientific experience. Not able to translate the interplay of matter and energy that serves as the cornerstone of the process view into a sense of the world as event, many are still overwhelmed by the scientific perspective. They adopt, therefore, the structural foundation of early science as their imaginative base. Structure becomes the cornerstone for approaching the world instead of force—be it the spiritual force of the supernatural, the energy base of the process, or the rhythms of nature in the romantics. And the implications of such a shift are significant. Psychologically the human presence on earth becomes dominating. Philosophically, probings about ultimate questions appear futile and irrelevant compared to the exciting power that rests in the hand of the collective human to shape the world for utilitarian ends. Religiously, there is less and less motivation or encouragement to see the human life as an expression that is qualitatively and quantitatively a small part of an awesome, majestic, and mysterious whole.

Psychologically, autonomy and utility become governing terms. Impressed by the power to alter structures, impressed by the causal accountability of structures, the popular mentality finds little need to measure human behavior by any preordained laws. As an autonomous creature, the human feels free to shape its life in whatever way it wishes. The question one faces in ethical decisions is a utilitarian one: What is the psychological, biological, and social impact of proposed patterns of behavior, and how do these impacts measure against the image of what one wants to become.

Philosophically, therefore, there is little motivation to probe the roots of human qualities. Decisions about human fidelity, truthfulness, drug stimulation, and environmental accountability are not in this view measured against given norms of either divine or natural origins. Rather, one must decide how one wants life to be structured and what are the effects of different forms of behavior in promoting given structures.

And finally, as for the state of contemporary religious consciousness, with the emphasis on the here and now that grows out of the focus on structure, there is little motivation to place the societal framework in a larger context. With the mechanical cause-effect accountability, there is little incentive to turn to greater powers as an explanation for the daily trials that face each individual. Religion is thus robbed of its single most important point of motivation. In other words, human survival and even its simple well-being is not seen as tied in with the dynamics of some greater whole.

Taken collectively, all these movements are part of a complex shift in human consciousness. They are usually grouped under the term "secularity," and as with any complex mosaic the term does not admit of an easy definition. Larry Shiner attempted to group various uses of the term as it is employed in measuring change within religions. He offers the following six possibilities:

1.   The previously accepted symbols, doctrines and institutions lost their prestige and influence. The culmination of secularization would be a religionless society.[20]

2.   The religious group or the religiously informed society turns its attention from the supernatural and becomes more and more interested in "this world."[21]

3.   Society separates itself from the religious understanding which has previously informed it in order to constitute itself an autonomous reality and consequently to limit religion to the sphere of private life. The culmination of this kind of secularization would be a religion of a purely inward character, influencing neither institutions nor corporate action, and a society in which religion made no appearance outside the sphere of the religious group.[22]

4.   Knowledge, patterns of behavior, and institutional arrangements which were once understood as grounded in

divine power are transformed into phenomena of purely human creation and responsibility.[23]

5. The world is gradually deprived of its sacral character as man and nature become the object of rational-causal explanation and manipulation. The culmination of secularization would be a completely "rational" world society in which the phenomenon of the supernatural or even of "mystery" would play no part.[24]

6. The culmination of secularization would be a society in which all decisions are based on rational and utilitarian considerations and there is complete acceptance of change.[25]

It is obvious, therefore, that different aspects can be stressed in working with the term. Placed within a spatial framework, one can see the secular model as promoting an outward direction. In contrast to urging one to relate to the higher forms of the spiritual world, or to exercise one's creative direction within the overall flow of energy, or to develop a rhythm with the pulse of nature, here one is confronted with a plastic world in which everything, including humans, can be altered provided one develops the proper techniques to shift the given physical structures. There are limits, of course. But these are limits that are dictated only by the biological and environmental structures.

The viewpoint, as Shiner develops it, does contain essentially the same points as those developed in this study. There is an emphasis on "this world" as an autonomous realm. Structures and values are of "purely human creation." The human adventure is challenged to deal with nature as "the object of rational-causal explanation and manipulation." The sense of mystery "would play no part": there are only unresolved problems. And finally "utilitarian considerations" become the governing factor for human behavior.

The question we now face is how these qualities are found

one would naturally expect to see it in the culture's popular art form. Indeed, quantitatively, films do seem to present the secular view more persistently than any other. Frequently, one finds in films characters presented in functionally defined roles—a detective, a lawyer. Film in general has a difficult time in developing character, working as it does within the general confines of ninety minutes. Thus, given the limitations of the medium, commercial films adapt rather easily to the secular mode by defining their characters within their vocational tasks.

Even when films attempt a deeper probing of character independent of explicit vocation, they frequently are true to the tenets of secularity. A case in point would be Homer Smith in *Lilies of the Field*. As he tries to present this self-reliant individual as an embodiment of secular man, Neil P. Hurley first quotes from Harvey Cox's *The Secular City*:

> Contemporary man has become the cosmopolitan. The world has become his city and his city has reached out to include the world. The name of the process by which this has come about is secularization.[26]

Hurley then goes on to state that Homer has a "fluid 'ego system,' pragmatic and quick to adapt to changing circumstances." He is seen in contrast to the German nuns, who operate from the supernatural model with determined, given norms for human behavior. Homer is willing to accept a wide variety of behavior in others. But his acceptance is not devoid of realizing the stubbornness of the religious superior or the prejudice of the Southern construction foreman.

Homer is pictured by Hurley as one who "creates his own work pressure and forges his own destiny." And he summarizes his character as "complete, harmonizing 'this-worldliness' with the religious sentiments of compassion, service, and sacrifice." He appears to be oblivious to any greater setting for the human drama. Homer is more interested in showing an immediate sensitivity to human needs and in exercising a practical effort in solving overt problems.

In a similar vein one meets Gene Garrison in *I Never Sang for My Father*. The son realizes that his father, Tom Garrison, has been formed by a hard, bitter struggle from poverty to reasonable wealth. The struggle has produced a hardness; the success has developed a smugness and an insensitivity. There is a hatred mixed into this chemistry as the old man has grown with a deep resentment for his father, who had abandoned the family. The son, Gene, realized how the older man, played by Melvyn Douglas, has been rendered unable to love in any advanced sense of the word. He in turn is struggling to keep alive in himself a human sensitivity and gentleness.

The father has dominated the son's earlier years and has shown little appreciation for the son's accomplishments as a writer and teacher. As Tom Garrison hated his father, Gene faces the same hate and realizes that, if he permits himself to feel this way toward the old man, he will in turn become bitter. Death ends a life, as he states at the end of the film, but not a relationship. There is never a question of a given right or wrong that must govern one's life. It is simply a matter of personal choice. This becomes clear in discussing his father with his sister or in the affair he has while engaged to another woman. There are many options opened to human behavior. One must settle on the life style by choice, not command. The only accountability is that one will become the way one behaves.

In *Lilies of the Field*, therefore, the film presents the secular hero—one who is governed by compassion and sensitivity to immediate needs, one who does not come to situations with a blinding set of principles, but who is able to adapt to the real needs of the people about him. Homer is one that the audience is led to admire because he has a competent command of his own life and does not allow the pressure of the situation to dehumanize him. Gene Garrison, by contrast, finds the pressures of the outer world as pressing him toward a life of hate. He does not control the situations as easily as Homer. He senses the complexities of life as far more intense. He does not simply win or lose at the end of the film. As with most struggles in life, neither victory nor defeat makes a clear claim.

There is a third movement that must complement these two films. It is found in Michael Ritchie's *The Candidate*. The film begins with a professional campaign manager walking away from a lost election. He has already singled out his next candidate—a young, attractive store-front lawyer who is fighting for the rights of the oppressed. Two ingredients make this particular crusader stand out. First, he has achieved some impressive results. Secondly, and more importantly, he is a member of the McKay family—a politically potent force in California politics.

In the opening sequence, one finds the young idealist suspicious of the prospects of running for the Senate. He likes his job and has a sense of personal accomplishment. But faced with the reality of what he can accomplish in his limited position against what the present conservative senator achieves in his influential office, he is convinced to run provided one ground rule is established. He is to be his own man, one who speaks straight on the issues.

Working in a party primary where there are few promising candidates, his blunt answers and honest doubts win the day. When faced with controversial questions that do not admit of simplistic answers, he is willing to admit uncertainty. When thrown explosive questions that alter the time-honored mores of society in light of newer social visions, he bluntly states his position as an attempt to let people honestly know what type of man they would be electing. His approach is new and refreshing and his opponents lack enough appeal. He thus wins by a plurality.

To this point, therefore, the young McKay has remained a man true to himself—a man after the mold of Homer. He is fluid enough to meet situations without too many blinding prejudices. He has a compassion and a sensitivity that enable him to meet the real needs of the present situation. He does not have any explicit world view that governs his decisions other than respect for all life forms. But the forces he meets in the general election are far superior and more overwhelming than any that the previous two protagonists encountered. The forces that he meets here are governed by the simple utilitarian goal of victory. Everything is shaped and formed by the end—including to some extent the young man of principle.

Entering the general election against a thoroughly entrenched, politically wise conservative, the young McKay finds that the dynamics are not the same as those of the primary. There is a session with an advertising group that will handle the media campaign. They study the spot commercials of the opponent and discuss the way the camera angle and distance coupled with the lighting and sound track project the proper image. This short course on film criticism makes the young candidate nervous. These media people are packaging him as a product. When he objects, the media managers assure him that he will have final approval over anything that is used.

Secondly, he has direct encounters with the incumbent. The blunt honesty that worked so well in the primary proves to be unfeasible in the realities of the general election. The candidate never makes any clear decision that winning is more important than principles. Rather, the question continually arises as to whether or not issues can be intelligently raised in a campaign. Each time McKay tries to surface complex issues he is made to appear ridiculous by his opponent, who realizes that one must package simple answers around the few issues that interest the generally apathetic public. The campaign

managers continually confront him with the choice of soften-
ing an approach here and covering over an issue there in the
name of presenting a more intelligent or identifiable position.
The options are generally put in the context of bending to the
nature of the political campaign to give him the opportunity of
working for the causes he really believes in or appearing as a
fool shouting to the wind in such a way as to bring disgrace on
what he truly feels. He has become a symbol for certain concerns in life, and if he proves ridiculous so will his causes.

There are not many well-made political films. This particular one does at times lack subtlety, but it does an admirable
job of showing how the external setting, the need to respond to
the practical concerns of the moment, can gradually act upon
the individual. The changes are subtle, but they are also
undeniable. When one finally steps back and looks at the self
as McKay does at the end of the film, the victory seems meaningless because he has changed. Without ever making an explicit dramatic decision, he did everything in the campaign he
vowed he would not. He looks at himself and discovers a different person. When his father greets him after the victory,
this man that epitomized everything that the son hated in
political life can shake his hand with satisfaction and tell his
son he is a politician.

The first film, *Lilies of the Field*, thus presents the secular
figure as hero in clear contrast to the supernatural figure. The
second work, *I Never Sang for My Father*, grasps the secular
as simply the factual dynamic in which one must develop
one's life. The final work seems to capture the more threatening aspects of such a setting. In doing so it does not promote
other visions of human development. It simply warns the individual of the threat that the present external situation poses.

E. The Depth View

I record these in the order in which they occurred,
without the slightest intention of commenting on their

possible meaning. I have never been particularly enthusiastic about the psychoanalytical direction. Yet I cannot deny that in these dreams there was something like a warning which bore into my consciousness and embedded itself there with relentless determination.[27]

With this introduction to the third dream sequence, Isak Borg echoes a long line of film characters whose search for their true self carried them somewhere into the depths of their person. There is Guido in *8½* who struggles against the centrifugal force of society that threatens to tear the self asunder. He cannot withstand the pressure on the simply rational level and only maintains a delicate balance in his inner space through a series of dreams and deliberate fantasies.

There is Rachel from the film of the same name. She is not important as a public figure such as Guido is, with producers, lovers, and newspaper reporters hounding her every move. She is, instead, a lonely, shy school teacher in a small, ignored town. Her life above the funeral parlor with her mother is filled with frustrations. As she reaches the halfway mark of her life in her thirty-fifth year, the drives of her inner self cannot be content with the measured existence into which she has settled. Similar to a later role Joanne Woodward plays in *Summer Wishes, Winter Dreams*, Rachel through her fantasy life discovers dimensions of herself that her conscious life could not admit.

This is the key to films which probe inwards. One cannot grasp oneself fully. One cannot accomplish enough in the societal reality to satisfy all that swells within. One must deal with these dimensions in ways other than the simply rational or face the prospects of eventual disorder or at best a life of continual negative tension.

This struggle is strongly present in Ingmar Bergman's *Wild Strawberries*. Isak Borg's life is almost at an end. He has many facets to himself that he simply blocked from his consciousness. But the secure conscious picture he has developed at the age of seventy-six has been achieved at a great price.

The film opens with Isak giving a rather pleasant account of his life, but this is contrasted to a sleep dream in which he finds himself on a deserted street in which the broken clocks seem to indicate that time has come to a standstill. He finds himself in a place where "the street seemed to be endless"and where he is "so cold that . . . his entire body shivered."[28] He then meets a faceless figure who crumbles to the ground as a dust-filled form. A second encounter comes as a horse-drawn hearse capsizes and the coffin springs open. As Isak goes over to investigate, a hand reaches out to pull him into the coffin, and he sees that the form is none other than his self struggling to pull him into the place of death.

This dream is similar to the "evil and frightening dreams which have haunted"[29] Isak for the past few years. And as he progresses through a daydream, another sleep dream, and a conscious attempt to fantasize, one learns much of Isak's makeup. Bergman is brilliant in the sensitive way he weaves the psychological fabric of this old man by interrelating the favorable conscious vision of himself with the brutal truth of the sleep world and the more modified revelations of the daydream. As Isak himself explains to Marianne after his second sleep dream, "It's as if I'm trying to say something to myself which I don't want to hear when I'm awake."[30]

Eventually Isak does face some truths about himself. Part of the transformation comes through the power of the day as he receives an honorary degree from the University of Lund, part through the strong encounter with his daughter-in-law, and part through the persistence of his subconscious. The transformation is not radical. It may not even prove lasting. But the closing sequences show that he is making a conscious attempt to be concerned about the lives of those near him—Marianne, Miss Agga, and his son Evald.

In this film there is no question of the ultrarational dimension of the self being harnessed by the rational faculties.

Rather, the film recognizes that the two dimensions are on a continuum and will eventually have an impact on each other.

This interchange which is suggested in rather subtle terms in *Wild Strawberries* is made more explicit in Fellini's *8½*. Here one encounters a famous film director whose creativity has run dry. He has started an expensive film production, but the story has not formed. He is looking for some inspiration that will enable him to focus creatively the many different parts of the story. Because he continually lies to his producer, his cast, his wife, and most others with whom he deals, there is a continual pressure from them for an honest commitment. First, the producer, who has spent large sums on lavish sets and expensive contracts, insists that the production can be stalled no longer. Secondly, the claim of the cast is embodied in an aging star who continually demands some information about her role. And finally the struggle to create a meaningful commitment to those closest to him is highlighted by the presence of both his wife and his mistress as well as the disturbing dreams about his parents. And there are, of course, the continual demands of the public embodied in the pursuit of the press.

Unlike Bergman's story where there is a conflict between the subconscious reality and Isak's conscious vision of himself, Fellini takes a slightly different approach. Guido, the director, finds in his dreams and fantasy life a fuller, stronger expression of movements that he has at least some awareness of in his conscious thought. Thus the film opens with a dream sequence in which Guido is caught in a massive traffic jam. He becomes entrapped in the poisonous atmosphere of the cars while those about him simply stare in passive silence. He finally achieves his freedom and flies above the crushing confinement of the social reality below only to find his ankle tied by a huge rope. He is suspended there like a kite for several moments and then finally falls to the earth.

As he is about to crash to the ground, he awakes. He finds himself in the treatment room of a health spa. The dynamics of the dream tells far more forcefully the plight of this famous director than the bits and pieces that one gathers from the controlled exchange with the doctor or later with the critic who has been hired to evaluate the script. He feels confined, almost imprisoned, by his inability to live up to the commitments he has made to others. Yet he is unwilling to admit failure. The result is a social reality that has little difference in tone or control than that of his psychic dramas. In both Guido has little ability to influence the course of events.

This interplay between both worlds sets the rhythm of the film. After his affair with his mistress, he falls asleep and has a dream. The feelings of guilt that gnaw at him in this psychic drama are grounded in his early life. The dream takes place at the grave of his parents. One soon realizes that the sense of loyalty and purity that his Catholic upbringing urged and which were so blatantly violated in this affair with his mistress are symbolized in his parents. They continually complain about the conditions of their tomb and Guido's neglect. In other words these are the first people whom he has been unfaithful to, and they are the primary symbols of this type of guilt. This relationship between his affair and his parent's tomb is even more logical when one learns that Guido sees his wife more as a mother than a lover. In one segment of this second dream his wife plays the mother's role. Later the association is reinforced in the harem sequence of the film. Guido consciously fantasizes about a harem where all the women of his life live in a community bound only by their admiration of him. Each plays a different role based on the aspect that most fascinates Guido, and consistent with the earlier dream the wife is seen once again as an embodiment of the purity and service of motherly love.

One realizes, therefore, that Guido's psychic life is a whole. The feelings of guilt because of his unfaithfulness to his wife are at one with his feelings of guilt toward others that he has neglected in life. Or taken from the perspective of love, the love that he feels for his wife is basically the same feeling that he had toward his mother. And just as he felt the need to find other relationships with women than those of a mother and son, he seeks relationships now other than husband and wife. The fact is, of course, that Guido to this point is a child or adolescent, and it is doubtful that he could have a mature, well-rounded relationship with any given woman.

Other themes are similarly developed. One sees how given feelings or ideas are present in the dynamics of Guido's conscious life; then one is shown how the given ingredient is woven into the greater fabric of Guido's psychic makeup. Thus one finds Guido is both fascinated and alienated by the Church as he has several encounters with one of Italy's cardinals. This meeting triggers in his mind the experience of awe and alienation that he had as a youth in the boarding school of his childhood. Similarly Guido spends time at a nightclub and participates in a mind-reading act only to relive the early fascination of his all-night vigil before a supposedly magical picture. In virtually every situation the social setting, though powerfully and visually embodied by Fellini, is complemented by a corresponding psychic movement. The movements range from the essential (the search for dramatic vision in his fantasies about Claudia) to the trivial (his hanging of the pedantic critic). But in each case the psychic reality appears as necessary to help Guido get some grip on his social reality.

Throughout the film Guido has created the centrifugal forces that threaten to pull the self apart by his refusal to deal with life in an honest way. His lies cause him continually to respond to the pressures of others who demand that he fulfill his promises. It is only when he takes the important step of admitting failure in his current film that he is able to take the first step toward directing his own life rather than living it in response to the pressures of others. This important step is taken at a news conference where his actions may be tantamount to professional suicide but are necessary for a personal rebirth. One never witnesses the social reality of the news conference. Rather, one is presented with its psychic enactment. Similarly when Fellini is faced with the challenge of integrating Guido's personality as a result of the newly found freedom, once again he turns to the psychic realm in the grand parade of characters where Guido takes charge of everyone in his life and causes all to work together in a grand parade. Guido is once again directing his life. Perhaps now he will be able to salvage his creative life by directing a quality film.

To an extent, therefore, Isak's and Guido's journeys are ones in which they seek to know themselves. That is a familiar phrase to most. People today want to know their true selves and presume that entails a probing of the subconscious. Contemporary Westerners are a psychological people trained in psychological terminology of various degrees of sophistication. They may or may not give attention to their dream life and their conscious fantasy. But they presume that dreams and fantasies are an acceptable avenue of activity and presume as well that persons must in some way go to the depths of themselves.

The attraction of this setting for film makers should be obvious. The conflict resides within one single character. The conscious self does not know the true self but suspects that something lurks at one's core. The story has many possibilities as the writer can give the tale a turn toward the abnormal, can leave it embodied in a normal self, or can leave the question in the balance as others react to the protagonist's inner struggles. In any case, the story can fulfill the task of drama by capturing in complete form that which is found incomplete in daily life.

The attraction for the religious concern should be equally obvious. The conflict between a false sense of self and a true sense of self that comes from the core of one's being has compelling religious potential. But it has been in large measure a potential that has not been fulfilled. Part of the hesitation has its source in the early movements of psychology. The best way, it was felt, to get to one's subconscious was through dreams. But there was always an uneasiness with translating the truth of dreams into the truth of rational thought, particularly with the supposed dependence on the expert psychologist who acted as the interpreter. The objective professional clearly had prejudices; and while the expert might offer some helpful suggestions, the interpretation was colored by the concerns of the profession.

Since the early decades of the twentieth century, however, psychology has matured. This maturation, coupled with a greater stress on the individual's ability to encounter fruitfully his or her own psychic life with some reward, opened at least a mild appreciation of the inward path as having religious potential. Lucy Bregman, in a helpful article, has tried to highlight at least some of the avenues currently being explored. She suggests four possible approaches. One she sees as represented in Harvey Cox's *Feast of Fools*. In this work Cox speaks of fantasy and focuses on its ability to picture alternate life styles and its consequent importance for a Western culture caught in a dreary world of possibilities. The emphasis here, of course, is not in pursuing the true self directly. At most there is an indirect search that presumes the self will express the inadequacy of modern forms by presenting alternate ones.

She next turns her attention to the Jungian approach, especially as found in his *Memories, Dreams, Reflections*. She sees this approach as trying to enable the individual to feel "connected with the peoples of the past without having to go through institutional channels or be actively aware of the 'public sphere!' "[31] In contrast to Cox, who saw the potential of fantasy as changing the social sphere, this approach to fantasy is seen as seeking self-completion in the midst of an indifferent world.

Thirdly, she turns her attention to two psychologists whose work has been done in a fairly recent setting—Singer and Klinger—and notes their relationship to the earlier work of Varendonck. These men, working in the traditions of experimental psychology, do not limit fantasy to the bizarre or the extraordinary. On the contrary, they would seem to support that much of fantasy life is concerned with the ordinary. She concludes from this position that "these thinkers do not make any global claims about the value of fantasy for modern men, since the function and contents of fantasies vary so greatly."[32]

Bregman seems to summarize this group in drawing from positions set down by Klinger. He argues that fantasy can have an effect on creative activity provided the fantasy is deliberately drawn upon; it is rich enough to warrant attention; and there is some reaction to the task at hand. The tone that Bregman sets to the discussion of these authors seems more positive. She apparently approves emphasizing the more limited potential of fantasy that stems from seeing fantasy as a more limited human activity. But perhaps Bregman is too measured in her assessment. What should not be missed is the importance of the background of all mental activity for the conscious whole. This is a point that Bregman does not give adequate stress. She is correct to criticize Cox, who is too ready to translate the movements of the psyche directly into the practice of social reality. But she appears to overreact when she responds to these writers. One cannot translate the psychic reality very easily, but it does serve as the background of conscious reflection. The relationship should be stressed to some degree.

Finally the article mentions what is termed "movements like Psychosynthesis and Gestalt therapy."It is shown how these movements make use of a combination of directed and undirected fantasies in attempting to deal with issues of one's person. The point stressed here would be the therapeutic effect of the fantasy itself with little reference to the need to translate or interpret the fantasy into the societal framework that was stressed in Cox or even Klinger.

Whatever the value of these different movements, several points can be made. First, there is a dimension of the self that cannot be dealt with on a simple rational level. The need for the therapy of sleep dreams is a testimony to this truth. Second, if one wishes to confront the religious dimension in its search for human relationship with the greater whole, then this unconscious self must be taken into account. Therefore, there will always be some concern with the inward journey of the third dimension. It will continue to have an attraction for stories, and it will continue to have an attraction for the religious dimension.

Joseph Campbell shows this basic sense of relatedness. First, he argues that the dynamics present in the great religions' basic myths and rituals are indispensable for the inherent movements of the self:

> Apparently, there is something in these initiatory images so necessary to the psyche that if they are not supplied from without, through myth and ritual, they will have to be announced again, through dream, from within—lest our energies should remain in a banal, long outmoded toyroom at the bottom of the sea.[33]

He goes on to make the connection more explicit while acknowledging the differences between myth and dream:

> Dream is the personalized myth, myth the depersonalized dream; both myth and dreams are symbolic in the same general way of the dynamics of the psyche. But in the dreams the forms are quirked by the peculiar troubles of the dreamer, whereas in myth the problems and solutions shown are directly valid for all mankind.[34]

Conclusion

This volume began with the presupposition that images are important for human thought. The second chapter has tried to suggest how films can create lasting images that would not be likely for most without the cinema experience. This present chapter has tried to suggest how images serve as the basis for any articulated sense of direction. Humans are spatial creatures and must orient themselves spatially before developed utterances can take place either in sequential word patterns or sequential celluloid patterns. If one accepts the contention that the religious sense of reality orients the human life to the life forces as a whole, then one can appreciate how a sense of direction found in an art form will be of serious interest. Finally, any sense of reality, as argued from Arnheim, will be projected in simple terms of forward, backward, up, down, in, and out.

The supernatural mode with its layered hierarchy to existence challenges the human life to make itself correspond to the higher governing forms if it wants fulfillment. The process model places the human life in an ever fluctuating process that entails an intricate interplay in all facets of the process that is interacting with a whole which is dependent on but not reducible to the sum of its parts. The secular context offers a picture of more isolated entities set by their outward structure while the depth model insists on a unique inner space that must be probed if one wishes to have an authentic existence. Finally, the romantic model is seen as the reverse of the process. One must go back to the pulsating source of nature if one wishes to attain an experience of fulfillment.

These directions are seen as basic. One can point to traditional theologians such as Calvin and Aquinas as operating within the supernatural framework. Whitehead and de Chardin have developed their religious thinking within the parameters of process. Bonhoeffer and Cox have identified with the secular thrust while Schleiermacher and Coleridge have worked with the dynamic of the romantic. Finally, Freud, Jung, and Campbell can be numbered among those probing the religious experience from the depth perspective. These models are therefore highly suggestive ways of approaching any serious probings of human identity. One can maintain that any serious probing of human life is at base religious. Or one can simply maintain these models as the point of common reference for the unity of all human thought.

A point of caution must again be stressed. To suggest that a model can be seen to dominate a particular film presentation is not to exclude other possibilities. When one is dealing with models, one is not dealing with logical exclusives. All models or potential directions reside in persons at once. One may fluidly move from one to another as so many different approaches. More often than not, however, individuals usually have one or two that dominate as the context of their thought. Similarly, in films, because of the discipline usually required in a dramatic presentation, there will be a focus on one particular approach over another.

Secondly, to speak of a given set of films as working from a given orientation is not to reduce them to one vision. Certainly there are many approaches to the division of dramatic presentations. Susanne K. Langer in her book, *Feeling and Form*, argues this in promoting her understanding of the underlying vision of comedy:

> To give a general phenomenon one name is not to make all its manifestations one thing, but only to bring them conceptually under one head. Art does not generalize and classify; art sets forth the individuality of forms which discourse, being essentially general, has to suppress.[35]

Notes

1. Rudolph Arnheim, *Visual Thinking* (Berkeley: University of California, 1969), p. 27.

2. Ibid., p. 31.

3. Thomas Gornall, "A Note on Imagination and Thought About God," in *A New Theology No. 1*, ed. Martin E. Marty and Dean G. Peerman (New York: Macmillan Co., 1964), p. 122.

4. Interview by D. Delouche, quoted in Gilbert Salachas, *Federico Fellini* (New York: Crown Publishing, Inc., 1969), p. 114.

5. The phrasing may be different from one traditional primer to another, but the thrust is the same.

6. William F. Lynch, *Christ and Prometheus* (Notre Dame: University of Notre Dame Press, 1970), p. 28.

7. James M. Wall, "Biblical Spectaculars and Secular Man" in John Cooper and Carl Skrade, *Celluloid and Symbols* (Philadelphia: Fortress Press, 1970), p. 53.

8. Gene Youngblood, *Expanded Cinema* (New York: E.P. Dutton & Co., 1970), p. 141.

9. Gerald Mast, *A Short History of the Movies* (New York: The Bobbs Merrill Company, Inc., 1971), p. 422.

10. Marshal Kinder and Beverle Houston, *Close-Up* (New York: Harcourt Brace Jovanovich, Inc., 1972), p. 87.

11. Youngblood, p. 139.

12. Alan Casty, *Development of the Film* (New York: Harcourt Brace Jovanovich, Inc., 1973), p. 383.

13. Mast, p. 422.

14. Kinder and Houston, p. 92.

15. Casty, p. 383.

16. Kinder and Houston, p. 92.

17. J. J. Saunders, "The Meaning and Evaluation of Romanticism," *Romanticism*, ed. John B. Halsted (Boston: D. C. Heath and Company, 1965), p. 3.

18. Irving Babbitt, "The Qualities of Rousseauism," in *Romanticism*, p. 11.

19. Karl Rahner and Herbert Vorgrimler, *Concise Theological Dictionary*, ed. Cornelius Ernst, trans. Richard Strachan (Freiburg: Herder, 1965) pp. 333–34.

20. Larry Shiner, "Six Meanings of Secularization," *Journal for the Scientific Study of Religion* 6 (Fall 1967): 207.

21. Ibid., p. 211.

22. Ibid., p. 212.

23. Ibid., p. 214.

24. Ibid., p. 215.

25. Ibid., p. 216.

26. Neil P. Hurley, *Theology Through Film* (New York: Harper and Row, 1970), p. 15.

27. Ingmar Bergman, *Four Screenplays of Ingmar Bergman*, trans. Lois Malmstrom and David Kushner (New York: Simon and Schuster, 1960), p. 284.

28. Ibid., p. 218.

29. Ibid., p. 219.

30. Ibid., p. 269.

31. Lucy Bregman, "Fantasy: The Experience and the Interpreter," *Journal of the American Academy of Religion* 43 (December 1975): 723.

32. Ibid., p. 733.

33. Joseph Campbell, *The Hero with a Thousand Faces* (New York: World Publishing Company, 1956), p. 12.

34. Ibid., p. 19.

35. Susanne K. Langer, *Feeling and Form* (New York: Charles Scribner's Sons, 1953), p. 327.

4

Religious Reflection, Films, and Stories

ALL reflection has one aim or goal. It tries to digest the flood of what often appears to be a chaos of experience. This digestion or consolidation is necessary if the person is to be capable of creatively responding rather than simply reacting to the situations encountered. The "I" center must be consolidated. The interior space must be developed and enriched if one is to have the strength actively to respond to situations and thus give direction to the self. That is the purpose of reflection in general. Our specific concern, religious reflection, works within this overall dynamic as it attempts to orient the self to the greater whole that serves as the context for all beings.

A life that does not nurture reflection, therefore, is one that can easily be overwhelmed when the routine or rhythm of a setting is upset. A life that does not nurture religious reflection in particular is one that is very susceptible to experiencing a basic disorientation as to the sense or purpose of human existence itself. To stress this need for religous reflection is not to champion simplistic answers, however. One who has adopted ready-made formulas in the religious realms is as susceptible to having the self crushed as one who ignores confronting the issue. There has to be a slow, mature absorbing of experience if the self is to achieve a rich texture and strength for its inner space.

Reflection in general and religious reflection in particular, therefore, are not trying to grasp the facts of reality. Human consciousness, as was argued in the introductory chapter, has reached sufficient sophistication to realize that it is not discovering the structure of reality as it is in itself. Rather, it is probing for insight through its systems of symbolic reflection. Huston Smith presents the case well:

> Specifications of life's meaning can no longer be considered verbal reflections of the meaning that inheres in life independent of our specifiying; they are not conceptual mirror images of a meaning that lies at hand, awaiting detection and description. Strictly speaking, we cannot *find* life's meaning; to a considerable degree at least, we must *construct* it. . . .
> From now on it is going to be difficult for man to regard any meaning he secures for his life as being objectively ingrained in the nature of things. He will see it as being, at least in part, a construct.[1]

While realizing this difference between the meaning that we construct and what exists "independent of our specifyings," it must also be asserted that the human is forever seeking intentional and organic relationships. As the title of Smith's book states, humans are *Condemned to Meaning*.

The question to face at this point is what role story plays in the quest for meaning. There are a number of issues that must be understood as basic contentions. First, one's initial experience is in some basic sense narrative in character. Secondly, the starting point of the human reflection that struggles with this experience is remembering, which in fact is a way of telling stories to oneself. And finally, a people must seal the fabric of the social fiber by developing stories that assure individual members that the vision of the culture is true. Once these points about story have been established, the implications for the film medium will be suggested.

The first challenge then is the claim that the initial conscious experience is, as Stephen Crites has contended,[2] narrative in character. It is seen as primarily narrative in that one receives it in units or sequences usually directed toward some emotional, psychological, or physical end. Frequently, one narrative is interrupted by another, and there may be a great deal of overlapping. Yet the quality of sequence, the context of time, and the objective of an end are well captured by the model of narration.

It is important not to become too restrictive in terminology. One might insist that the dynamics of narrative or story are not captured in the above movements. But to the extent that they are an adequate description (and there would seem to be strong common threads), conscious experience is seen as being captured by the metaphor narrative. As the term is used here, therefore, "narrative" implies some order. Yet the order can be minimal. Reflection is needed to firm the order or meaning both of one's conscious experience and of other movements of one's person to the extent that one is able to surface them to the conscious level.

To speak of this need for reflection is not to demand that all become abstract philosophers. Highly abstract thinking has a unique value, but it is not the most basic or necessary form of reflection. The simplest form of reflection is remembering. Remembering is the form that most closely resembles the initial experience and is likewise essentially narrative. But one narrative (remembering) is not a simple repetition of the other (experience). As has been argued in several places in this volume, all narratives have a purpose and goal which color the story. One remembers to satisfy a mood or some highly formed purpose; and therefore, one does psychological surgery to the initial experience depending on the dynamics which trigger this remembering.

What is being argued, then, is that remembering is the most

basic form of reflection and that people usually remember in the form in which they experience: a sequence of events marshaled toward an emotional, psychological, or physical end. In short remembering occurs in the form of a narrative or a story. But remembering is not to be seen in some dictatorial relationship with the other forms of reflection. All have indispensable roles to play in achieving the integration of the self.

This struggle to grasp intentional and organic relations must take place on many levels within the individual. While the initial experience is received in sequence, the reflective powers often stop the sequence and lift out a particular image (the face of a loved one, a room in which one grew up, an alley in which one played, or a country setting) or even juxtapose images from different phases of one's life. These are reflective moments with little overt conscious drive. But remembrance can also be a deliberate, directed activity of the individual. Whether it is highly intentional or not, such reflection is effective in integrating, particularly the emotive levels of the individual.

Within the human, of course, reflection takes on a much more abstract character. One can work with patterns of sound called music and sift out the commotion of a particularly hectic day by working through a musical composition. On the other hand, one may use patterns of highly abstract words in attempting to discern patterns to one's experience. In any case, the more abstract the form of reflection the more one is dealing with general themes and is, therefore, trying to discern larger movements in a life rather than absorb a particular expression. Such an assertion in no way means to draw strict categories. The reflective life is a whole. But this demarcation simply attempts to nuance different dynamics in given forms of reflection.

It is precisely because the reflective life is a whole that one must not presume that one can simply focus on a single dynamic of reflection to the detriment of others. If any one area is neglected, the "I" suffers. Not to have an integration or to have an unimaginative, confining integration at any one level of one's person hinders the whole person. Likewise, the integration one achieves at one level (one's hopes) must be in keeping with the integration effected at another level (one's mind).

To translate into more specific terms: There are many people who have life logically structured. They have set answers for the flow and ebb of human experience. They have, in short, achieved an integration at the level of mind. But their life also attests to the price they have paid for such a synthesis. There is an obvious tension between one level of the self and other levels, for the mind has not dialogued with the emotive dimension. The mind believes, but the heart does not.

Conversely, those who have achieved some degree of emotional integration may have done so at the expense of serious thinking. They represent the individuals mentioned previously who are able to achieve a balance as long as the movements of life remain within given rhythms. But once these rhythms are upset, then the individual is lost for he or she has not developed any larger perspective.

One can graph the above comments as shown on the following page:

Conscious experience as narrative

All reflection influences initial
experience

| | Memory | Juxtapose Image | Particular Image |

Private
Reflection: Abstract   Music
              Thought

The public influences the
private

| | Narrative | Poetry, Film | Painting, Sculpture |

Public
Reflection: Theology   Music
              Philosophy
              Psychology

Reflection for insight →

Insights that enable the I to integrate

The graph, of course, goes beyond the comments about private reflection. It introduces its relationship with public reflection. Sculpture, painting, narratives, music, philosophy, theology—all are seen as common forms of reflection that correspond to individual activities. Like their private parallels, the more particular the public reflection, the more it is addressed to the emotive life. Again, such an assertion in no way means to draw strict categories. The greatest sculptors and painters without a doubt affect the mind. To say a painting primarily presents an idea, though, is as unacceptable as judging the artistic accomplishments of a film by its theme.

Of course, stories are judged basic to a people's reflection. They give "a coherent picture of what exists, what is important, what is related to what, and what is right."[3] They achieve what Gadamer claims for all art: that in art is "produced and brought to the light what otherwise is constantly hidden and withdrawn."[4] But while Gadamer is correct in ascribing this function to all art, stories must be given a unique place. Stories are an important step forward in achieving a stability and texture for a people, for they have the ability to introduce a cohesive world view with a minimum of violence to the particulars of life. Such a cohesive force is necessary for a stable society. The more particular art forms, on the other hand, have only a limited potential to achieve this integration, while highly abstract forms of reflection are more the result of a cohesive society than the cause.

As with one's private stories, the public stories shared by a people are not a simple reflection of order, but to some extent create it. Smith's constructs of meaning are as applicable to the public sphere as to the private. No form of human reflection can be simply objective, and narratives are no exception. This principle is brilliantly dramatized by Doris Lessing in her novel *The Golden Notebook*. She shows how even the simplest event is altered by the inner dynamics that must be created in a story. Even in her blue notebook, Anna, the struggling protagonist, is doomed to a "false account" as she tries to list the blunt, factual events of a short segment of her life.[5]

But such limits on reflection need not be portents of doom for the human struggle attempting to grasp that of which it is a part. It is merely a restatement asserting that the human knows symbolically. If one holds that symbols harness that which the human encounters, then—because a culture's story cannot be seen as merely reproducing reality—the question one must address to the culture's story becomes, "What degree of insight do its symbols produce?"

Within the limited scope of this chapter, therefore, the first three concerns laid out in the opening pages have been addressed: the narrative quality of experience, the element of story in remembering as our most basic form of reflection, and the role that story plays in developing the social fiber. Attention must now turn to the role film plays within these given dynamics.

First, considering it simply as a medium, film juxtaposes images in a continual sequence. As with the juxtaposing one does in private, this causes certain objects to be assimilated in a variety of ways, depending on the sequence in which they are placed. The process is similar to that in which an individual attempts to assimilate a new place of residence. Gradually through the continual contact with the living space as well as comparisons with former residences, one becomes acclimated to the new surroundings. Similarly, in a film one receives possible new orientations to objects as they are placed in a variety of film sequences.

Film, therefore, as a medium of images possesses a particular potential for the emotional reflection of a people. But films are not simply a series of images. Most film forms have as their primary end the telling of a story. And as audiovisual stories they have a tremendous potential for confronting the human on many levels. In fact, this multiplicity is probably why they have such an appeal as a popular art form.

They can assimilate both the individual's initial experience and the basic form of reflection as well as work from the integrating stories that serve the fiber of the society. To a degree this is true of any story form. But film's immediacy becomes its superior edge. It does not rely on abstract word patterns as does, for example, the novel. For most, this offers greater impact. Film, therefore, has a special power for telling stories to a large group of people.

In trying to account for this power of films, Gadamer can once more be of help. He speaks of the "ontological value of pictures." He insists that a picture is not simply a copy but "affirms its own being in order to let what is depicted exist."[6] As a result, he positions the picture "equipoised halfway between a sign and a symbol." He continues with the following statement:

> Its representative function is neither a pure pointing-to-something, nor a pure taking-the-place-of-something. It is the intermediate position which raises it to its own unique level of being.[7]

Film narratives, then, usually tell their stories partly through the sequence of words in the dialogue, partly through the sequence of pictures that are "equiposed halfway between a sign and a symbol," and partly through the sequence of music. When all three of these forms combine to produce a single impact, one can begin to appreciate the power of films to seize their audience.

Again, such arguments are not to ignore the limits of film in comparison to other forms of storytelling. After speaking of the ontological potential of pictures, Gadamer goes on to speak of the "borderline position of literature" where "apparently there is no representation that could claim an ontological value of its own."[8] The important term is "apparent." For Gadamer insists that at base the power of literature rests on the same grounds as the power of other art forms. In fact, one could extend the argument by developing the inner dynamics of literature and suggest its potential for greater tensive richness. There is in fact, though, little value in trying to speak of one medium as better than another. The purpose here is simply to focus as strongly as possible on the dynamics of film in order to sensitize the reader to its potential impact of human reflection.

Film, therefore, has unique powers as a story form. But once this is said, there is a barrier to treating specific film stories. Film stories cannot be reduced to analytical written words. They have a uniqueness that must be to some extent violated in any such translation. Anyone who has read lengthy descriptions of film is aware that reading about films one has not seen or will not have the opportunity to view has little value. Film reviews may prove helpful for one sorting out the impact a film has had. In a more questionable context, reading about a film prior to viewing may help orient the individual and thus sensitize one to dimensions of the film experience that would ordinarily be missed. But abstract discussions or lengthy descriptions of unviewed films can be a tedious and limited experience.

At any rate, to get involved in long discussions about specific stories in film would simply be a diversion from the stated purpose, namely, to offer general categories for investigating the relation of film and religion. But if one does not wish to get involved in particular stories, can one group stories under general headings? In facing a similar question in *Stories to the Dark*, William James O'Brien had said, "Stories are infinite in number, but they tend to constellate in correspondence to certain modes of imagining."[9] That in fact was the implied position of the previous chapter. But one must be careful not to violate the integrity of specific stories in an attempt to detect their common threads.

There are no simple solutions to these pitfalls. As reflective beings, humans feel the need to talk about their stories. But the barrier to translation is inherent in the forms. Realizing this dilemma, it is necessary to limit the remaining comments to some general cautions against the consolidating movements of the previous chapter. The difference between the two presentations is primarily one of emphasis. It must first be insisted that no film can be reduced to a single movement; rather—discovering the underlying construct as was done in the previous chapter—it is more the case of unveiling the dominant movement. Second, even within the dominant movement, the potential for stories must be regarded as unlimited.

In coming to grips with the first question, then, it must be realized that to relate successfully the direction implied in religious thinking with that present in films, it is not necessary to bring to film the consistency of view one would discover in disciplined verbal presentations. One can simply discover the roots of a particular vision in the dramatic presentations of a film.

The previous chapter was correct, for example, in insisting that in both *8½* and *Wild Strawberries* the dominant movement of the films is toward the level of being that lies beneath immediate consciousness. There is a reaching inwards. In the former, Guido is continually expressing the depths of himself through sleep dreams, daydreams, and conscious fantasy, as is Isak in Bergman's film. But Guido is a public figure, and the outer world of society is an important element in the film. Its power is partly represented in the centrifugal force that tries to obliterate him. Most of the sets, as is the rule in a Fellini film, are the wide-open spaces of beaches, large monastery halls, health spas, public baths, huge public theaters, or vacant hotel lobbies. They do not allow a sense of orientation, and the continually moving camera captures the sense of aimlessness that one meets in social and business encounters.

Likewise, in treating Isak, one cannot deny that the challenge is from without as well as from within since Isak refuses to allow others to penetrate his life. The living death that has gripped the old doctor has a long history, as he has held his childhood sweetheart, his wife, his children, and his parents at a measured distance. While he must journey within to be confronted by his true character, he must journey without if he is to find any salvation. Once again the film cannot be reduced to a single direction.

These examples lie, of course, within a given world. Perhaps the point could be made more forcefully by comparing heroes who embody two different constructs, but who must compromise within the common sphere of the social world. Thus Don Carver, played by W. S. Hart in *Tumbleweeds*, is a clear embodiment of the romantic hero. He stands in obvious contrast to Pasolini's portrait of Jesus in *The Gospel According to St. Matthew*. The two could be contrasted in the following way:

W. S. Hart	*Pasolini's Jesus*
1. loves the earth	1. world renouncer
2. nostalgic for the past	2. projects toward future
3. rugged individualist whose main virtue is his naturalness	3. social reformer
4. leaves others to their ways	4. calls for a radical transformation in lives of others
5. victory in the end	5. defeated in the world he renounces; victorious in the world of "reality"
6. victory is external so external violence is permitted	6. victory is internal, violence on this level permitted
7. victory is achieved through inward style and grace	7. victory comes primarily through inward grace

These characters differ from Guido and Isak in that they embody different constructs. But they are also heroes as opposed to protagonists. As such, one would expect them to promote a sense of direction much more forcefully. And they do. But, like the two previous individuals, they must come to terms with the social structure. Hart's character must compromise the romantic figure. Like the tumbleweeds that once blew free over the plains but are now caught in the taming barbed-wire fences of the Oklahoma Territory, Don Carver is corralled into settling down to married life on a ranch. But it's not half bad, for Miss Milly is quite a girl.

Similarly, in Pasolini's film, Jesus is a clear embodiment of the supernatural construct. But he too reflects the film maker's concern for the social order and acts as an instrument for social reform. Pasolini has enough integrity to give the spiritual struggle full reign. But such a concern does not have to be developed by ignoring the other complexities of life.

A supernatural hero who has concern for the social dimension and a romantic hero who comes to terms with society should present themselves as logical contradictions. But it is precisely here that one meets the difference between the rigidity and purity of analytical thinking, on the one hand, and the complexity and richness of stories. There is value in both approaches. But most feel more at home with the latter, for stories capture the dominant movement of their life.

It should be obvious, then, from the discussion of these four films that the importance of the imaginative constructs developed in the preceding chapter is not being summarily dismissed. Likewise, in arguing the second question, to insist that many variations can be played off a single construct is not to deny the underlying structure. One can speak of the romantic vision, for example, and still appreciate the infinite movements it can encompass: the noble savage, the ills of technology, the beauty of romantic love, the limits of the mind over emotion, the importance of the individual over society, the particular versus the universal, and many more.

In point of fact, in developing each of the constructs in the previous chapter, several alternatives were carefully suggested as forms for story development. Yet speaking of forms giving rise to forms still works within the process of categorizing. This is precisely what should be deemphasized. The argument is that stories cannot be simply compartmentalized, at least without an equally strong movement that emphasizes their uniqueness. And no general work such as this can develop the uniqueness of powerful stories. It can only suggest.

Conclusion

The interest of religious studies in stories is widespread. John Dunne, Sam Keen, Harvey Cox, James Wiggins, and David L. Miller are just a few who have recently dealt with the story form in general works of religious studies. They are indebted to those who have worked in the broader field of religion and literature and reflect the advances made in closely paralleled studies. To mention their names is to ignore the vast amount of work being done in specific fields of religious research, particularly scripture studies. But such a list does suggest the tremendous interest in the relation of stories and religious reflection.

There are those who will dismiss such a surge to the cult of faddism. But a more accurate reading would seem to be a maturing in the sense of expression. Stories have always played an important part in religious consciousness. But they have been placed in a secondary position to rational theology. The whole tension between rational thought and other forms of expression is a familiar one that has been extensively treated. Suffice it to say here that none of the responsible religious thinkers who promote stories do so at the expense of other forms of reflection. They simply appreciate story as a basic form of human reflection that might be moved to the forefront, given the dynamics of the culture. Rather than worry about some campaign to enthrone story in a place of eminence, a more serious concern should be detected in the danger of religious thinkers adopting the sense of story too easily. As Ted L. Estess has cautioned, to take a simple notion of story and to superimpose it in a simple way on life would be as disastrous as any dogmatism. Estess cautions that to imply "that story is by itself an adequate metaphor for interpreting human experience is to obscure the complexity of life under the rule of an aesthetic form."[10]

What has been argued in this chapter is that the metaphor of story or narrative captures many of the movements of human experience in general and reflections in particular. It also captures the specific design of most films. Story is thus an important point of contact for religion and film studies. First, because humans do embody their encounters with the greater whole in stories, they serve as the basis for the rhythms of life. Secondly, there is an important point of contact with films because humans do not manufacture their stories in a vacuum but draw upon the story environment, of which they are only partially aware. One must look at the stories in the popular forms of a culture to become sensitized to the stories of one's life.

Notes

1. Huston Smith, *Condemned to Meaning* (New York: Harper and Row, 1965), pp. 42–43.

2. Stephen Crites, "The Narrative Quality of Experience," *Journal of the American Academy of Religion* 39 (September 1971).

3. George Gerbner and Larry Gross, "Living with Television: The Violence Profile," *Journal of Communication* 25 (Spring 1976): 176.

4. Hans-Georg Gadamer, *Truth and Method* (New York: The Seabury Press, 1975) p. 101.

5. Doris Lessing, *The Golden Notebook* (New York: Simon and Schuster, 1962).

6. Gadamer, p. 124.

7. Ibid., p. 137.

8. Ibid., p. 142.

9. William James O'Brien, *Stories to the Dark* (New York: Paulist Press, 1977), p. 4.

10. Ted L. Estess, "The Inenarrable Contraption: Reflections on the Metaphor of Story," *Journal of the American Academy of Religion* 42 (September 1974): 433.

5

Film Criticism as Establishing Sequence for Religious Studies

THE liberal arts tradition acknowledges the interrelation of academic areas of study. There is, however, a strong cultural and professional tendency to keep the disciplines well defined. Putting aside the appropriateness of this insistence, one who involves other humanities in a religious studies department is usually challenged as to how the study deals with theology, the religious question, religion, faith, or any of a variety of other traditionally accepted terms. One may insist that theology deals with a self-revealing God through a sacred scripture or a church tradition. Another may distinguish between the theological question of a self-revealing God and a broader religious question of primal thinking about the Being of beings. A third position may contend that this primal thinking must be directly related to a religious tradition before such an investigation can rightly be termed religious rather than philosophical.

The basic contention of this volume has been that the religious question deals with the living relationship between human life and the life forces in general. As the introductory chapter insisted: "The religious sense cannot exist if there is no identity with a greater whole." Following from this orientation, chapter 2 dealt with film as a medium of particular images and their potential interaction with religious consciousness. Chapter 3 addressed itself to the question of the more general imaginative constructs and the implication that these spatial orientations have for film and religious awareness. And finally, chapter 4 attempted to relate the religious dimension and films to the extent that both employ stories. This chapter, therefore, seeks to extend this line of reasoning to the study of film critics. If there is a genuine overlap between religious consciousness and film articulation, then many of the questions that the film critics confront should have at least implied importance for the religious concern.

The film critic's job is, of course, to consider the ingredients of the film experience. But to probe the nature of film as an art, one must probe the nature of man as a reflective being. To probe the nature of man as a reflective being is to probe the identity of man and the awareness that constitutes that identity. This mutuality is true whether one is studying the effect of the film on the audience or the aesthetics of the film. The concern here will be to consider the major contours of modern film criticism and then use these to expose the mutuality of film art and religious consciousness.

A. The Film and the Audience

In considering the audience and the film, one might begin with a work by Alan Casty, *The Dramatic Art of the Film*. He examines the effect of the audience on the film as well as the effect of the film on the audience. He speaks of how the cinema must take into account the identity of the audience:

All of our contemporary art has been affected by changes

in the structure of our feelings, especially by changes in our ways of looking at and defining reality—both internal and external. Certainly any account of the ways that the film works in expressing its human content must be placed within the context of these changing ideas about the ways in which human consciousness works and the ways in which all the arts work.[1]

Casty obviously feels that in studying film one gets some idea of the changes in the society to which the film is directed. This imagery could hold true of all art forms; but as we have argued in the previous chapters, it is particularly true for the film since it is a popular art form and captures the contours of imagery as it rests in the popular culture.

A more specific comment is found in Robert Gessner's work where he speaks of the "nervous need" in a modern audience and the import this has on dramatic forms.

Psychologically astute receivers of stimuli perceive relationships that would have been lost a generation earlier. The visual-minded seek structural relationships in fresher forms than the dramaturgy of Shakespeare or the mosaics of Mozart. Accelerated time satisfies a nervous need for the unexpected. The tempo has been rising through the years.[2]

To appreciate the above point, consider a film of the 1960s such as *Two for the Road*. The camera continually cuts from one point to another in the marital history of a couple, portrayed by Albert Finney and Audrey Hepburn. Only the dialogue allows the viewer to grasp the relationship between the various settings and the various scenes. The camera rests on a given setting only occasionally to catch its breath. Even in this commercially entertaining film one must have a certain sensitivity to the modern flux and confusion in human identity today.

This film, of course, is one chosen for its techniques, but seldom does one find any camera in modern film resting very long on any given scene. The change in pace is certainly evident when modern techniques are compared to a film made in the 1930s such as *Ninotchka*. Here the camera is quite content to sit and watch Greta Garbo and Melvyn Douglas hold a conversation about some of the niceties of life. The camera sits and watches two talented people go through accepted social rituals in a way that is complimentary to the social rituals. There is camera movement, but it remains mostly invisible—at least by today's standards. Today, insofar as any camera is willing to allow two people to converse, it will probably be busy doing its own acting as it moves from the hands, to a cigarette, to a statue. It will pan, zoom, soft focus, deep focus, and attempt to contrive some unorthodox moves because the niceties or the expected is not important. The culture has been fractured, and there is a "nervous need" for the unexpected in the hope that it will satisfy.

These are good examples of the type of questions film analysts must investigate when considering how films are received by an audience and how in turn the culture has a direct bearing on the types of film that are produced. To the extent that they must probe the basic images of a culture, their findings have a direct importance in discovering a people's religious position. As argued in the previous chapter, one does not formulate the imaginative backdrop of religious consciousness in a vacuum. It is drawn at least in part from the cultural setting.

There is another aspect to this interplay, audience and film. Turning the perspective around, one can see that the study of film does not simply reflect changes in a people but promotes them. Casty quotes the French critic Charles Dekeukeleire, "If the senses exert an influence on our spiritual life, the cinema becomes a powerful ferment of spirituality by augmenting the number and quality of our sense perceptions."[3] The individual is thus made more aware of the texture, rhythm, and variety of the life expressions around and thus will have his or her identity in the context of these life expressions strongly affected.

Critic Béla Balázs agrees. In the medium of the cinema, he argues, one can discover things that the unaided eye could never grasp. He speaks of the camera unveiling the "soul of objects," "the rhythm of crowds," "the secret language of dumb things."[4] In other words, as argued in chapter 2, one who has viewed the filming of nature in which, through time-lapse photography, a flower blossoms, or through the telescopic lens, observes the activities of a bird's nest, sees things that could never have been observed without the camera. Likewise, one who has seen a film such as *A Thousand Clowns* could not then feel the same in a large crowd walking in one of the metropolitan centers; or one who has viewed films such as Pare Lorentz's *The River* or *The Plow That Broke the Plains* would have a transformed view of nature and man's activity in it. The camera thus makes available sources of consciousness that had not been available prior to the film.

Even if I am present at every shot, if I look on as every scene is enacted in the studio, I can never see or feel the pictorial effects which are the results of camera distances and angles, nor can I become aware of the rhythm which is their outcome. For in the studio I see each scene and each figure as a whole and am unable to single out details with my eye.[5]

What he is saying is an extension of an earlier argument. Philology tells us that words not only result from feelings and concepts but that the converse is true. If the word gives rise to feelings and concepts, how much more could new visuals, which are much more closely related to the emotive life of men, give rise to new states of consciousness?

Balázs does attach an additional note. He holds that the audience actively views a film because he feels there is a natural tendency to seek patterns and directions. Balázs comments: "Our mechanism of idea association and our imagination will always tend to put some meaning into such a meaningless conglomeration, even though perhaps only in play."[6]

What these previous comments mean for any primal think-ing about Being or the hermeneutics involved in transmitting any religious tradition is clear. First, if films have had to restructure themselves to meet what Casty refers to as "changes in our ways of looking at and defining reality" or what Gessner terms "structural relationships in fresher forms," then one would expect to learn something about the changes that have taken place in a people's structure of their basic organizing images. If the "dramaturgy of Shakespeare and the mosaics of Mozart" present conflicts with pictures, phantasms, and relational organizations out of which a people articulate, so also would the religious expressions that grow out of the period of these artistic geniuses. Certainly one does not ignore Shakespeare, Mozart, or the richness of Western culture's religious heritage. But one must also develop alter-nate expressions. Thus the mutual study can benefit both film and the religious heritage as they listen to each other. Put in terms of our present argument the film critics can present a number of helpful areas for pursuit by religious thinkers.

Secondly, inasmuch as films present a dimension of beings not open to human experience prior to film, this new ex-perience is bound to transform one's sense of oneself and the basic relationship to Being in general. It is precisely at this point that the film critics can sensitize religious thinkers to some of the parameters of visual extension present in films. More will be said on this point in investigating the realistic school of film criticism.

B. Realism and Film Theory

Film theorists note, therefore, how films reflect and affect the audience—its identity, values, and structures that emerge from these values. They speak of the power of the film to shape the human identity because of the power of the medium. The audience and the film mutually enrich or impoverish each other. The study of one reveals much about the character of the other. In putting this relationship to the religious question one can see that the religious concern can learn much about how the human identity is shaped, what shapes are present, what forces the human identity takes into account, and the images in which these forces are expressed.

The above concern of film theorists is not the main focus of film theory, however. Film critics do not generally give direct attention to the audience. Rather, they focus prime attention on the making of films and the nature of the projected image. The audience is frequently implied in the discussion but not the main point of attention.

Realism and expressionism are the two common divisions in considering the nature of the projected image. Two subdivisions of the latter which deserve special attention because of their historical importance are the auteur theory of film and the avant-garde theories of film. The first major division concentrates on the film as a creative focus of reality while the second accentuates the film maker's use of the film as any other artist would use his material to convey an individual vision of reality. The first is an objective presentation; the second, a subjective interpretation.

For realists, the naturalistic is the prime subject for cinema. Some develop rather exclusivistic theories and maintain that the only proper use of film is as a reflector of reality. Two such theorists are Siegfried Kracauer and Cesare Zavattini. A third who takes a strong realistic approach, though from a somewhat different perspective, is André Bazin.

Kracauer, in his book *Theory of Film*, conveys the thrust of his observations in the subtitle: *A Redemption of Physical Reality*. He looks upon film as saving, rejuvenating, enlivening reality by awakening the senses to what is present and helping the individual see that which the naked eye would have missed. This is not to say that Kracauer does not recognize expressionistic films as having been made. He traces them back to Méliès, who in contrast to the news films of the Lumière brothers, made films of individual fantasy and trickery. But he sees such films as an aberration of the true direction cinema should take.

Kracauer would have a great admiration for the Eisenstein of *Potemkin*, but less enthusiasm for such films as *Alexander Nevsky* or *Ivan the Terrible*. Much of the formalism that caused Eisenstein trouble with the Soviet film industry in the 1930s and 1940s is the very thing to which Kracauer also objects. In defense of Kracauer, however, it must be said that he does see the film maker as doing more than simply recording. One who creatively works with the camera brings to attention what was present but missed by many and would have been lost in history. As Giannetti notes:

> To redeem something is to recover it, to rescue it from oblivion. Even realistic movies, then, go beyond everyday life in some way: they show us things that we might not notice in the chaos and flux of everyday life.[7]

Eisenstein redeemed the drama and force of objects that were present in the Soviet revolution and which would have been lost.

Roy Armes, in commenting on Kracauer, notes that while the book was published in 1960, the main attention of the work rests with the films of the 1930s and 1940s. In citing *Greed, The Grand Illusion, Pather Panchali*, and *Potemkin*, Kracauer can easily build an argument. But in ignoring the later Antonioni, the later Resnais, the post-*Dolce Vita* Fellini, and Godard, he fails to challenge his theory. It would seem almost defenseless to dismiss the development of cinema that is represented by these films as aberrations of the film medium. An unbiased viewing of these works must justify them as valid and desirable visual celluloid expressions.

Another who presents a radical theory of cinema realism is Cesare Zavattini. As one of the most successful scriptwriters for the movement known as Italian neorealism, his attitude has understandable artistic origins. The thrust of his comments can be seen in a passage quoted by Armes: "Make things as they are, almost by themselves, create their own special significance. Life is not what is invented in 'stories.' Life is another matter."[8]

Sociologically, the setting of Zavattini also makes his attitude understandable. Faced with the breakdown of society and the rampant poverty of postwar Italy, he works out of a natural repugnance for withdrawing into the private or fantastic when the immediate needed so much attention.

While Kracauer suggests the importance of the "slice of life" cinema, Zavattini speaks of natural time as being absorbing in itself. As Armes quotes:

> While the cinema used to make one situation produce another situation, and another, and another, again and again, and each scene was thought out and immediately related to the next (the natural result of a mistrust of reality), today, when we have thought out a scene we feel the need to "remain" in it, because the single scene itself can contain so many reverberations, can even contain all the situations as we may need.[9]

Thus, Zavattini's theory would seem to direct him toward the undramatic development of time. But his work after the articulation of his film theories in the 1950s does not carry out his arguments.

Finally, mention will be made of André Bazin. For him the film is different from the other arts because for the first time reality can be produced without the intervening hand of the artist. A machine produces reality as it is. The cinema is important for what it reveals of reality and not what it adds to reality. This is the same basic stress found in other theorists but with a rather strange emphasis on the mechanical reproduction of the image. Kracauer spoke of the redemption of reality; Bazin speaks of the revealing quality of the cinema.

Cinema has greatly freed the other arts, Bazin argues. Having satisfied the basic human need to reproduce reality, film allowed the other arts to pursue a task for which they were better equipped—"the expression of spiritual reality wherein the symbol transcended its model."[10]

He continues:

> In achieving the aims of baroque arts, photography has freed the plastic arts from their obsession with likeness. Painting was forced, as it turned out, to offer us illusion and this illusion was reckoned sufficient unto art. Photography and the cinema on the other hand are discoveries that satisfy. once and for all and in its very essence, our obsession with realism.[11]

The film maker, Bazin continues, may have "something of his personality" reflected in the work, but he leaves this statement undeveloped and concentrates on film as differing from other arts, which "are based on the presence of man," whereas film benefits by his absence.

With all the stress on the objectivity of the film found in these three theorists, however, they do see the film as revelatory of man. This is a natural connection that grows out of the implied relationship of man's identity and his surroundings. Kracauer states in another of his works, *From Caligari to Hitler:*

> Inner life manifests itself in various elements and conglomerations of external life, especially in those almost imperceptible surface data which form an essential part of screen treatment. In recording the visible world—whether current reality or an imaginary universe—films therefore provide clues to hidden mental processes.[12]

Realist theories are also found in more modified form. Ernest Lindgren is a case in point:

I suggest . . . the film medium . . . demands a higher standard of objective realism than the other representational arts. This means that where the film director presents us with a realistic scene in a realistic manner he should as far as possible create the impressions he desires by what might be seen in actuality. This is not calculated to discourage imagination, on the contrary: the image arbitrarily brought in is an easy evasion of the problem. The hallmark of a good film style, as of a good literary style, is its objectivity.[13]

Without taking sides in the argument about what the essence of film should be, one can derive some of the potential for religious studies in the insights of this school of critics. They clearly point to the power of film in awakening the jaded perception to the objects or beings which it encounters. Kracauer speaks of the "Redemption of Physical Reality" as well as the "Inner life manifesting . . . itself in conglomerations of external life." Giannetti points out that film can "show us things . . . we might not notice in the chaos and flux of everyday life." And Zavattini notes that "things as they are . . . create their . . . own . . . significance." In his eyes realistic films can overcome a mistrust of reality.

While one may feel uneasy with any purist theory of film, the close affinity of many films to the physical contours of which one is a part is evident. Inasmuch as one's primal reflection about Being does not posit an opposition or distinction between Being and beings, the sensitivity created by a critic's work with films can greatly intensify awareness of the presence of the Being of other beings. If one is not faced with a rejection of the immediate reality in favor of another reality as is the case in various Occidental and Oriental religious traditions, but instead sees a unity to all expressions of Being, then film and the sensitizing by the film critics to the celluloid experience can prove to be a valuable vehicle for what has been traditionally called "grace."

The individual, in other words, must draw from the Being of beings. One can only do this through an awareness of the presence of Being. Whether this presence is initiated by Being, as some would have it, or by beings, there must be an awareness. At the very least the appropriate sensitivity to the depths of one's being and the being of others must be the usual precondition.

C. Expressionism and Film Theory

The last section attempted to present not only what one might term "polarized realist theories" but also those critics who simply see the film as a more realistic art than older forms. This group stresses, in other words, the strong affinity between the film and material objects. But this association does not blur an appreciation of the subjective element in the cinema. Balázs, for example, accentuated the relationship between what the camera records and the physical properties of things as they are found in reality. He might serve as a point of transition, therefore, between the realists and the expressionists, for he appreciates both perspectives. He insists that one cannot simply ignore the subjective element in the cinema despite all the realistic origins of its shooting. He argues: "The free, individual possibilities of the set-up brings about in the image the synthesis of subject and object which is the basic condition of all art."[14]

He recognizes that a shot is "saturated with the tension of a latent meaning which is released like an electric spark when the next shot is joined to it."[15] Thus he speaks of the subjective quality in every shot—the stress found in an expressionist such as Arnheim—as well as the creative freedom in the arrangement of shot sequence—the stress of the expressionistic Russian theorists with their emphasis on montage.

Balázs points out the major difficulty with realist theories by charging that films which simply concentrate on bare facts become the "most unreal, the most abstract."[16] It is not sufficient to present things as they are because things are always in relationship and in a field of perception. The one working with the camera must choose the field. Balázs summarizes in the following way:

> For any object by itself alone is always a withdrawal from reality, because without explanatory references to one another the things of reality are not real, things being not only themselves but at the same time links in chains of events and causalities.[17]

What the writings of Balázs, therefore, represent are those theorists who recognize the realistic-expressionistic polarity as two aspects of the film. It is much like the form-content question that faces every film theorist whether discussing Ford, Hitchcock, Antonioni, or Fellini. The form and the content are one. But to speak of them in the sequential ordering of words requires that one attempt to divide the living whole of art into several conceptual aspects.

Those who try to develop any exclusivistic theory of film art allow their theory to prejudice their appreciation, for such an approach succeeds only at the expense of ignoring a larger number of creative artists. Stephenson and Debrix are correct in insisting on the deductive approach. They argue that what is good and bad in film "must in the ultimate analysis depend on what the best individual artists have done."[18] Just as the rules of grammar are derived from what is recognized as good writing, so the rules of film making should be discerned from the good films that have been made.

There are, however, critics who write from a strong expressionistic stance who present rather persuasive arguments. The two to be noted here are Rudolph Arnheim and V. I. Pudovkin. Both insist on the distance of the film from reality for slightly different reasons and from slightly different starting points.

Rudolph Arnheim is one trained in gestalt psychology and places himself in what he terms the Kantian turn of the school in which

> the most elementary processes of vision do not produce mechanical recordings of the outer world but organize the sensory raw material creatively according to principles of simplicity, regularity and balance, which govern the receptor mechanism.[19]

Since Arnheim's psychological perspective stresses the interpretive character of all men's impressions, one would naturally expect him to stress the interpretive character of the camera as used by the film maker. Arnheim argues that the film is an art form because of its distance from realism, which allows the film maker a greater creative interpretation. This is why he argues against the artistic contribution of sound, which brought the film closer to reality. In a similar way he attacks the wide screen, which destroyed "the last pretense of a meaningful organized image."[20]

Arnheim thus stresses the subjective character of the individual shot as the result of the interpretive expression of the director. He does not deny the added creative possibilities that an expressionistic writer such as Pudovkin would place on montage. But he feels the Russian theorists were guilty as others in failing to capture (as Eisenstein eventually did) the interpretive character of each shot.

A few subtitles found in his work give the key to his view of film making. He mentions: "Projections of Solids Upon a Plane Surface," "Reduction of Depth," "Lighting and the Absence of Color," "Delimitation of the Image and Distance from the Object," and "Absence of the Space-Time Continuum." These terms capture Arnheim's vision of the film maker molding the plastics of his image to convey his personal vision in much the same way that any painter or sculptor would. There is an infinite number of impressions to be made and a wide scope of shapes to be molded.

While Arnheim had his theory heavily influenced by gestalt psychology, V.I. Pudovkin developed his ideas of montage in the Russian film-making experience shortly after the revolution. His work with Kuleshov and the experiment with the facial close-ups referred to in chapter 2 show the origins of his regarding the film maker as one who works with celluloid strips in much the same way that a painter works with oils.

Pudovkin, while stressing points different than Arnheim's, does arrive at basically the same conclusion: "Between the natural event and its appearance upon the screen there is a marked difference. It is exactly this difference that makes the film an art."[21] He does not see the film as being "shot." Rather, he puts stress on the building of shots not from the raw material of nature, but from the raw material of celluloid.

Arnheim and Pudovkin are expressionist theorists who hold to the extremes of this view. There are likewise more moderate expressionists. These individuals would emphasize the subjective character of film making, but hold back from prescribing a formalistic pattern for films.

Stephenson and Debrix in the work mentioned earlier, *The Cinema as Art*, are a good case in point. They clearly acknowledge that Arnheim's approach serves as a "starting point"[22] for their theory. But they also insist that their "modifications and additions are considerable."[23] They give recognition to the realistic character of cinema, which they claim "gives us more of physical reality than other art."[24] But they definitely come to the point of insisting that film does differ from physical reality. Like most expressionistic theorists, they argue again that it is the difference which gives the film its power.

In statements that echo to some extent the subdivisions of Arnheim's work, they emphasized in the space-time continuum of the film and reality different variations. In their eyes, what the film maker must do is give the audience "a feeling of reality like that created by a natural science."[25] The camera through an unguided recording of things could never create "so complete an illusion" with which the artistic possibilities of the film must begin.

Another rather curious approach to the expressionistic character of film is found in Roy Armes's book on Italian neorealism. He notes that the meaning of the term "realism" itself is difficult to agree upon. In his study of Italian neorealism he quotes several of the movement's leading directors. Roberto Rosellini states: "Everyone possesses his own realism and everyone thinks that his own is best." Visconti argues: "Neorealism is above all a question of content." But Fellini disagrees: "Neo-realism is not a question of what you show, its real spirit is how you show it."[26]

Armes does not want to argue that there is not a movement called "neorealism." But he does wish to bring out that a movement such as this is a complex expression that must accommodate numerous approaches. Such a position clearly notes that "realism" itself is open to the subjective interpretation of the film makers. This is what leads Armes to argue the following:

> For this reason the realist film maker must have the qualities of an artist able to select and prove, disentangle the real from the feigned, order the over-abundant material, in a word be able to give it formal expression.[27]

In evaluating realist theories, one cannot deny that the camera produces celluloid images closer to their objects than other art forms. But in trying to take this position one step further, one runs into impossible difficulties. A revealing contrast at this point is to take Bazin's position on the mechanistic reproduction of the camera and to see what other theorists deduce from it. Marshall McLuhan, the media theorist, starts with this mechanistic character of the film and insists that the mechanism leads to an illusion stronger than any other art form. He states: "But the film form is not a pup-

petlike dance of arrested still shots, for it manages to approximate and even to surpass real life by means of illusion."[28] He
argues that mechanistic production is always on the verge of
bringing the objects to life, a different type of life than the objects possess on their own. As a result, one encounters a "sur-
realism of dreams" and not the raw stuff of reality.

The Auteur Theory

Some mention should be made of the auteur theory of film,
which is a form of expressionism. It deserves attention
because of its role in focusing on the individual styles of directors long ignored by film critics. The movement is generally
seen as having its origins in the magazine *Cahiers du Cinema*
in the mid-1950s. It found a forum in magazines such as *Film
Culture* in this country and in the writings of critics such as
Andrew Sarris.

While recognizing the contributions of other technicians,
critics of this approach concentrate on the director as author
of the film. The important question for them is "how" a film
is made and not "what" the film is about. It is again the question of form and content. The "author" is appreciated
because he brings to the film a style that is identifiable and
unique. Because the film maker is working in a visual medium
and not a rational one, the style of visual composition is given
more emphasis than the "thoughts" that a film might suggest.
The approach of the auteur critics to the director has many
similarities to the critic's approach to the painter or sculptor.
A film must have a visual vitality and an absorbing movement
first in much the same way that a painting is considered for its
color composition and balance.

While opponents of this school generally appreciate these
critics for calling attention to the cinematic talents of such
men as John Ford and Alfred Hitchcock, they are appalled by
what appears to be a championing of the "in" directors'
poorer works and the ignoring of some of the difficult facts

that call the dominating influence of the director into question.

Giannetti, for example, can appreciate the attention that the auteur theory has focused on Ford's *Stagecoach*, *My Darling Clementine*, and *Fort Apache*. While a synopsis of these works shows them to have what might appear to be exhausted themes, Giannetti feels that the treatment in a film such as *My Darling Clementine* reaches the realm of an epic which celebrates the "diverse culture that went into making America."[29] Yet he is quick to echo André Bazin, founder of *Cahiers du Cinema*, in bemoaning the a priori judgments found in auteur critics in which any films made by the chosen directors were praised. He terms "bizarre" the championing of what he calls "competent technicians" such as Raoul Walsh, Nicholas Ray, and Vincente Minnelli over "major artists" such as John Huston, Elia Kazan, and Fred Zinnemann.

With their stress on style, the auteur critics do run into some telling ironies. In a book such as Ivan Butler's *The Making of a Feature Film*, which gives a feeling for film making from several perspectives, one cannot help appreciating the contributions of many technicians to the film process as well as the ignorance of many directors of some of the most important aspects of style—lighting, lens, simulated effects. Graham Petrie in an article, "Alternatives to Auteurs," hits this point strongly. He notes something that was true of all studios: frequently a director had little idea of the film as a whole and at times did not direct important scenes of the film—a case in point, the railway station scene in Welle's *The Magnificent Ambersons*.[30] In their tendency to single out Hollywood directors, the auteur critics actually pick some of the least independent of the film makers. What they might be focusing on is a point Eisenstein noted in speaking of Russian cinema: namely, the creative possibilities found by working in a highly organized system.

For all its problems, however, the auteur theory perceives a truth worth noting. It is a fact that a number of outstanding directors do have a noticeable style. This style may arise from the creative team that the more successful director tends to assemble about him. But the main thrust of the theory, once one has put aside some of its extremes, is that if a director has a major control over a production, he will show his influence. If he assembles a poor team of actors, script writers, cameramen, and film editors, the final work will be poor. If, on the other hand, the director has a subsidiary role to the producer or a studio, then his hand will be less evident. The contention of the auteur theory must be criticized by the facts of production and the results of the distributed work. He who has power has power. That which is artistically impressive is artistically impressive.

Avant-Garde Theories

Finally, there is a third form of expressionistic theory that has contributed to and grown out of avant-garde films. More than any other approach to cinema, this view holds the film to be the expression of an individual film maker's vision. The extremes to which these theorists take their contentions are understandable. They concentrate on what could be termed "radical films." They do not attempt to apply their contentions to commercial, mainstream productions. Some would simply write off the film of the general public as aberrations of the art form.

Generally the avant-garde film makers reject the idea of a film as imitation. They do not seek to reproduce in their films and frequently do their most to keep an audience from slipping into such an illusion. Secondly, they reject film as a representation of things; they seek the representation of feelings—the feelings and visions of the artist.

There is an affinity, therefore, between the avant-garde films and the art-for-art's sake found in other arts. Just as a painter might use his canvas upon which to place patterns that emanate from him, so the film maker uses celluloid strips. It is precisely this tendency which Balázs criticizes so strongly. He argues:

> Soon, however, this school, known in European cinematic art as avantgardism, developed into a separatist art-for-art's-sake toying with mere form and ceased to exercise the fructifying influence it had at one time possessed and which manifested itself, for instance, in inspiring and developing to an important art form in its own right such things as documentaries and "films without a hero." . . . The possibilities of the means now determined the ends, and the formal intentions the content. This trend, consistently followed, leads to the final logical conclusion of a form giving itself its own content, of words devised to designate not things but merely other words; that is, to frustration and emptiness.[31]

Balázs follows this strong note of caution with a clear statement of the contribution made by avant-garde films. He recognizes the creative experimentation present in these works and finds their influence on general film making undeniable.

Actually the movement is not so simple as some of its descriptions would have it. There is a variety of trends and styles that any movement which stresses subjectivity must have. First, there are those films which attack film illusion with a vehemence. Film techniques may be deliberately misused "to call attention to themselves."[32] Scratchy films may be used, lettering may appear between shots, microphones may be present, cameras may shoot cameras. Two names which Ken Kelman associates with this tendency are Bruce Conner and Stanton Kaye.

Secondly, Kelman speaks of those film makers who try to present undressed reality. They project it in all its undramatic qualities, attempting to avoid the interpretive presentations of accepted documentary practice. The most obvious figure in this style would be Andy Warhol, who gives a look at sleep in *Sleep* and eating in *Eat* and "more complex" material in *Screen Test* and *The Chelsea Girls*. But once again this leads to the difficulty of any bold line drawing between reality and illusion.

Kelman comments:

> And the very fact that no "realistic" *effects* are striven for gives to Warhol's hyperrealism an illusionistic quality, that which life itself gives when contemplated with absolute unwavering focus; an undeviating concentration that old cinema never conceived, since such purity is indeed a negation of the "reality" (illusion) principle. In short, the border between illusion and "reality" is not clear enough either in life or in the cinema of absolute realism to satisfy the old standard.[33]

Finally, Kelman notes a third trend which reverses Warhol's staring at the externals and thus attempts to project the internal states of the film maker by ignoring recognized externals. The names associated with this style are Stan Brakhage and Carl Linder. Brakhage's films are described as avoiding "rigid preconceived 'truths,' " and working instead with "images correlative to immediate personal conceptions." The example cited is the hand painting of patterns on film of his child's birth. The patterns strive to capture the experience of Brakhage at such a moment. They do not simply focus on the event. The event does not serve as the context for the personal experience. The personal experience is the informing context for the event.

Kelman does mention a fourth category which is in many ways simply an extension of the third. Light is the "substance and subject." The objects of reality are ignored completely as in Tony Conrad's *The Flicker*.

It is in the writings associated with these avant-garde films that one sees the most direct association with the religious question as first stated. This is to be expected. Since this is the film form that most clearly sees the film maker projecting his personal questions, one would expect avant-garde film to be the film form that addresses itself most directly to the problems of human identity. One therefore hears Jonas Mekas stating:

> Our movies are like extensions of our own pulse, of our heartbeat, of our eyes, our fingertips; they are so personal, so unambitious in their movement, in their use of light, their imagery. . . . There is pain in the arts of the last few decades. The whole period of so-called modern art is nothing but the pain of our ending civilization, the last decades of the Christian Era. Now we are looking, we are being pulled by a desire for something joyful deep within us, deep in the stress, and we want to bring it down to earth so that it will change our cities, our faces, our movements, our voices, our souls—we want an art of light.[34]

Similarly, the necessity of the personal quest is clear in books such as *Expanded Cinema* by Gene Youngblood. He begins the first section with the following statement:

> As a child of the New Age, for whom "nature" is the solar system and "reality" is an invisible environment of messages, I am naturally hypersensitive to the phenomenon of vision. I have come to understand that all language is but substitute vision and, as Teilhard de Chardin has observed, "The history of the living world can be summarized as the elaboration of ever more perfect eyes within a cosmos in which there is always something more to be seen."[35]

When Youngblood speaks of "expanded cinema," he insists that he is not concerned with "a movie" at all. Expanded cinema is "a process of becoming, man's ongoing historical drive to manifest his consciousness outside of his mind, in front of his eyes."[36] The reason audiences seek entertainment in film is to escape a life style in which the intention of man is not given opportunity for expression in the external. When life and art become one, then "life becomes art." There will be no need for the specialized genres of the arts.

From the perspective of religious studies, therefore, one sees this school as promoting the visions of the film makers. Balázs remarks that "without explanatory references to one another the things of reality are not real." Arnheim starts with the basic position that "elementary processes of vision . . . organize the sensory raw materials creatively," and insists on the creative element of the film. Pudovkin argues that "between the natural event and its appearance upon the screen there is a marked difference," while McLuhan suggests that film "manages to approximate real life by means of illusion."

As they approach film, these critics are not saying that the cinema is simply another way of projecting an opinion. They clearly recognize the uniqueness of film while stressing that it must have a creative vision as must any art form. If this position be true, one must appreciate the role of art in a religious tradition. One of the functions of religion is to serve as a communal way in which one can deal with the basic issues of the self. The hopes, fears, joys, and anxieties of life are acted out in a context that provides a perspective and a salve to the human struggle. In one sense religion can be termed the public imagination, from which one can draw to organize an intellectual and emotional perspective on life. When one is living at a cultural juncture in which the public imagination is fractured, then art forms can supplement the images of one's private imagination by making available the creative integrations of artistic geniuses. Religion generally draws heavily upon the arts. However, in a time of cultural confusion, the relationship may not be supplemental as is frequently the case during cultural consolidation. But where there is the plurality of searching, the arts can be a definite complement.

The importance of film in this schema is that few art forms have the attention and power that films have in the public forum. Inasmuch as film critics sensitize the audience to the creative organization present in films, they can aid the searching religious imagination by putting it in contact with complementary imaginings that attempt to digest the newest movements in the present culture.

Most films do not have the burning statements that are implied by Mekas and Youngblood, but they do present some way of dealing with the issues of life. Even if deficient in their intellectual grasp, they capture an emotional resolution. The human is in need of integration on all levels of its being.

Notes

1. Alan Casty, *The Dramatic Art of the Film* (New York: Harper & Row, 1971), p. 2.

2. Robert Gessner, *The Moving Image* (New York: E. P. Dutton & Co., 1970), p. 312.

3. Casty, *Art of the Film*, p. 14.

4. Béla Balázs, *Theory of the Film* (New York: Dover Publications, Inc. 1970), p. 47.

5. Ibid., p. 46.

6. Ibid., p. 119.

7. Louis Giannetti, *Understanding Movies* (Englewood Cliffs, N. J.: Prentice-Hall, Inc., 1972), p. 189. The basic approach of this chapter is indebted to this work. It does not include all the possible approaches to the film criticism, but it does capture the major movements.

8. Roy Armes, *Patterns of Realism* (New York: A. S. Barnes and Company, 1971), p. 169.

9. Ibid., p. 171.

10. André Bazin, *What Is Cinema?* (Berkeley: University of California Press, 1967), p. 11.

11. Ibid., p. 12.

12. Siegfried Kracauer, *From Caligari to Hitler* (Princeton: Princeton University Press, 1947), p. 7.

13. Ernest Lindgren, *The Art of the Film* (New York: The Macmillan Company, 1963), p. 96.

14. Balázs, p. 89.

15. Ibid., p. 118.

16. Ibid., p. 175.

17. Ibid.

18. Ralph Stephenson and Jean R. Debrix, *The Cinema as Art* (Baltimore: Penguin Books, 1965), p. 23.

19. Rudolph Arnheim, *Film as Art* (Berkeley: University of California Press, 1958), p. 3.

20. Ibid., p. 5.

21. V. I. Pudovkin, *Film Technique*, trans. Ivor Montagu (London: George Newnes Ltd., 1933), p. 58.

22. Stephenson, p. 32.

23. Ibid.

24. Ibid., p. 33.

25. Ibid., p. 35.

26. Armes, p. 183.

27. Ibid., p. 24.

28. Marshall McLuhan, *Understanding Media* (New York: Signet Books, 1966), p. 256.

29. Giannetti, p. 200.

30. Graham Petri, "Alternatives to Auteurs," *Film Quarterly* 26 (Spring 1973): 27.

31. Balázs, pp. 156-57.

32. Ken Kelman, "The Reality of New Cinema," in *Film*, eds. Allen and Linda Kirschner (New York: The Odyssey Press, 1971), p. 104.

33. Ibid.

34. Jonas Mekas, "Where are We—The Underground," Kirschner, p. 110.

35. Gene Youngblood, *Expanded Cinema* (New York: E. P. Dutton & Co., Inc., 1970), p. 45.

36. Ibid., p. 41.

6

Religion and the Use of Films

THIS volume has been careful not to equate the film and the religious experience. They are seen as two distinct human endeavors. What it has been contending is that both deal with basic human movements and therefore influence each other as they meet in the human person. Film can affect religious consciousness. The religious consciousness of a people affects the films produced by a given culture. Given this basic relationship, either form can, of course, explicitly use the other for its intended ends. Certainly, films have used religion as the basis for their drama, particularly if religion is used in a broader sense. Religion has also used film in its attempt to create given convictions or states of consciousness within its peoples.

This concluding chapter will seek to offer a rationale for the explicit use of films in religion programs. The previous chapters have indicated obvious potential use. This chapter seeks to make a more explicit statement; in that sense it acts as a concluding segment.

To place the discussion in the context of the volume a reiteration of the earlier formulation of the religious concern should be made. The religious question deals with the identity of the self in relation to the life forces that contribute to and challenge the existence of the self. Secondly, any form that absorbs a large portion of a society's conscious time will affect the self's perception of its context. In a similar way, any medium that presents to the self realities that would otherwise be absent must naturally be of concern to the religious quest.

The above assertions, in a modified form, could be made of any art form. They are particularly pertinent to the film, however, because it is the most exposed art of the present period.

In a more specific sense the relationship of religion and film can be seen through a discussion of three major religious exercises. Religion, in its attempt to foster the mutuality of the self and the life forces, attempts directly to nurture the individual identity through communal prayer and private prayer. Secondly, it attempts to aid the individual through an articulation of the institutional identity which serves as a guide for the individual through its positing basic beliefs and translating these beliefs into doctrines. And finally, it attempts to foster the individual identity in relation to the immediate social setting through its community-oriented programs. These three phases of the one task may be termed the "spiritual identity," the "thematic identity," and the "social identity." The first is the self in solitude; the second, the self in reasoning dialogue with a primary community; the third, the self in encounter with the society at large. The remaining pages will speak of religion and the film in terms of these three facets of religious identity.

A. The Film and the Spiritual Identity

Traditionally, prayer has been divided into thanksgiving, adoration, petition, and contrition. In the first, one seeks to appreciate and acknowledge indebtedness to Being. In the second, the individual opens to grasp the awesomeness of Being. In the latter two a person seeks either to implore Being for further strength or to bemoan the callousness and insensitivity for past benefits. All four are, of course, different expressions of the one attempt to identify within oneself the Presence that the religious consciousness posits to Being as a whole. Most religions divide these prayerful probings into two general methodologies: public and private.

In fostering the spiritual identity of the individual, religion organizes the outward community prayer in its liturgy. The liturgy as an outward form of celebration attempts to foster the sense of presence characteristic of the particular religion. Generally the liturgy will be designed to influence the congregation through a variety of external forms—music, sculpture, painting, architecture, interior design, dramatic readings, and group dynamics. The aim is to create an organic experience which will make the community's perspective of the living expression present to the congregation. The human is one who needs the concrete to celebrate and to keep intense any existential entity. Friendship dies without some external means of renewal. The Presence shared by some community will also die if it is not given external expression.

Complementary to the liturgical prayer of the community is the private searching of its members. Most religions recognize the need for the individual to withdraw into a solitude to encounter the life forces according to the self's peculiarities. This solitude may be guided through official prayers of the religion or it may be left to the interplay between the individual and the expressions of Being that speak at a particular moment. Frequently, however, even at these most private moments the importance of externals is undeniable. The one in meditation may retire to a desert, a cell, a chapel, a rock garden, or some other place of quiet. The individual may choose the quiet of predawn, the solitude of late night, the rising spirit of early morning, the strong stare of noon, or the calming lull of the setting day.

In any case the externals are generally realized as important. The communal prayer recognizes the value of creating expression to act upon the individual and to invite the individual. The meditative prayer recognizes the need to listen to the silence, but usually the silence must be amplified through appropriate acoustics. As any veteran of prayer realizes, however, one should not keep the distinctions too great.

Given this dependence on externals in the spiritual quest of the community, the film in its more traditional as well as in its more experimental expressions offers a clear opportunity. If dramatic verbal communication is used, if the rhythms of sound, of painting, of interior design are used, why should not the drama of the film and its rhythms of images, light, and synchronated sound be used? Such heightened awareness enabled by heightened sensory experience such as those provided by film cannot be offered all the time certainly, but it is the function of liturgy to find a creative variety to aid its participants. If the film critics of all bents are correct in insisting that film presents views of reality (either by the process of recording or the process of creating) that would not otherwise be possible, then how can the prayer life of a congregation deliberately cut itself off from such an expression?

If a film maker such as Mekas speaks of his films as "extensions of our pulse, of our heartbeat, of our eyes, our fingertips," then this is a source and challenge just as any testimony is to the prayer life of a religion. If Youngblood, who is sensitive to an "environment of messages," finds that he is "naturally hypersensitive to the phenomenon of vision," could not a community of prayer possibly be stimulated by these messages? The film maker, in other words, may either be consciously trying to promote a personal testimony or may be simply interacting with the medium to convey some feeling or drive within. At any rate, the task is similar to the one Joseph Conrad set for himself in the 1897 preface to *The Nig-*

ger of 'The Narcissus': "My task which I am trying to achieve is, by the power of the written word to make you hear, to make you feel—it is, before all, to make you *see*. That—and no more, and it is everything." D. W. Griffith expressed the same sentiments less eloquently: "The task I'm trying to achieve is above all to make you see."[1]

If film does as Dekeukeleire claims, "influence . . . our spiritual life" through "augmenting the number and quality of our sense perceptions," does it not have an affinity with the spiritual quest of religion? If it does prod the audience, as Balázs notes, "to put some meaning in such a meaningless conglomeration," then certainly this can be a beneficial exercise to many in their attempts to awaken their religious consciousness.

B. The Film and the Thematic Identity

A religion, at least a Western religion, attempts to give rational expression to basic positions about the life forces. Thus a Christian religion might hold that the inherent good of man (image of God) coexists with the inherent evil in man (original sin) and project the eventual victory of man (resurrection) that is made possible through the intervention of the life forces (redemption) after a long and tedious struggle (sanctification, justification). It attempts to give these basic positions some articulation in cultural terms either in a random way or through a devised methodology (scholasticism, neo-orthodoxy, process thought). The basic goal of this thematic expression is to help the religion's members clarify their thinking about their identity as it derives from the religious community in a given cultural setting.

In an attempt to formulate rational perspectives or to theologize in an appropriate cultural way, a religion must continually search for the pulse of the times. Conscious experience is the raw material of reason. This experience is received in units or sequences directed toward some emotional, psychological, or physical end. Reason attempts to discover and articulate persistent or consistent patterns in that experience. In religions the official reasoning attempt is generally called "theology." Theology, therefore, like any rational endeavor, cannot ignore art. Art forms generally give the patterns of conscious experience articulation before these patterns are abstracted and given rational expression. The emotive character of art places it closer to experience than the more detached reasoned probings of man. Art frequently serves as an intermediary for reason. Historically one can see art capturing the spirits of a culture before they are given any impressive reasoned formulation.

Film as one of the art forms closest to the heartbeat of present culture is an indispensable consideration for any intellectual theologizing. Kracauer, Armes, and Casty all point to the film in its form and its theme as reflecting the nuances in values, structures, and other facets of human identity. To grasp, for example, the "nervous need" of a people, one would have to study its expressions in numerous areas. But certainly the study should include the film.

The more cinema causes or aids a people to discover things they could not on their own, the more it is necessary for the intellectual arm of religion. Theology cannot ignore the input that only the camera can make. Process theology, for example, cannot ignore the process unveiled by microscopic photography, the process of the bodies of the universe captured in cosmic photography, or the process in more immediate nature captured in delayed photography. They are new experiences and must take their place by the side of the experiences possible to man prior to the film.

C. The Film and the Social Identity

An institutional religion seeks to position its people within a perspective toward the world. Insofar as it does not definitely renounce its social setting as something to be shunned, it encourages a participation according to its self-identity and attempts through this social action to guide the relational posture of its members. Religions presently within the mainstream of the Christian movement generally encourage participation within society's activities. Even those which do not must face a general population which is present-oriented and looks upon the working of the present culture as important.

To the extent that its congregation attends films, a religion must both learn from and use the medium. McLuhan and others have removed any doubt as to the influence of the media over an individual's sense of reality. What is the precise relationship between a medium such as film and an audience's value system is, however, open to question. Two terms of Herbert Gans might serve as some help. He speaks of "the Hypodermic Theory" and "The Selective Perception Theory."[2]

The first of these sees the audience as basically passive viewers who are generally manipulated by what appears before them. Presented with a particular style of behavior, the viewer, while perhaps not adopting it as his or her own, will at least use the viewed way of life as a vicarious experience that will feed one's dreams and attitudes. To this extent the film may keep the audience passive in an immediate social situation, but in anesthetizing the audience, it will affect it and perhaps be impetus for long-range mutations.

The second approach sees the audience viewing a film with a set frame of reference. As I. C. Jarvie points out, in this case "the mass media perform the social function of reinforcing people's prejudice and blind spots, rather than enlightening and correcting them.''[3] The audiences either selects from a given film what agrees with its own position or it views only those films that it feels reinforces its position.

Another way of presenting this same dichotomy from a slightly different position can be found in an article by Gilbert Seldes, "Media Managers, Critics, and Audiences." Writing primarily from the perspective of television, he discusses how "given" is an audience. Here in part are the alternatives he lists[4]:

Either

Audiences exist
Audiences=public
Demand precedes supply
The public gets what it wants
Wants are specific

Or

Audiences are created
Public audiences
Supply creates demand
Audiences take what is offered
Wants are general

If the film reflects the tastes and values of a majority of the population or only the segment of the population that attends, then certainly a religion must study this form. If, on the other hand, audiences are made and their value system is affected by what is offered in the available films, then the religion must be equally concerned in its study of the film, its use of the film, and in its desires to influence the film.

Notes

1. Both quotes in Robert Gessner, *The Moving Image* (New York: E.P. Dutton & Co., 1970), p. 19.

2. I. C. Jarvie, *Movies and Society* (New York: Basic Books, Inc., 1970), p. 102.

3. Ibid., p. 103.

4. Gilbert Seldes, "Media Manager, Critics, and Audience," *Sight, Sound and Society*, eds. David Manning While and Richard Averson (Boston: Beacon Press, 1968), p. 41.

Appendix: Some Unique Questions About Television

In this volume "film" has been used in the broadest sense of the term. While important distinctions can be made between media such as theater films and television, there are far more similarities than differences. Both work with images and sound, both develop their presentations within some organizing constructs, and both deal primarily with stories. The first four chapters, therefore, are applicable to both forms. Even the section dealing with the film critics, whose primary interest is theater films, has many applications to television. There are, in short, far more similarities to the two media than differences. But this brief appendix will call attention to some unique realities of television.

Some of the contrasts between the two media are rather subtle. Marshall McLuhan has done much to surface some distinctions with his emphasis on hot media and cool media. Film is seen as a hot medium in that it "extends one single sense in 'high definition.'" The shot, in other words, is "filled with data."[1] In contrast, television is characterized as a cool medium in that it "leaves much more for the . . .user to do than a hot medium."[2] The one is seen as seizing its viewers and presenting its impact in a concentrated way. The latter is seen as having "low definition," which allows a casual participation.

Other differences have been stressed. In an article that attempts to compare television to a dream sequence, Marcus G. Raskin focuses on how both radio and television present a disjointed picture of their events as they intersperse commercial messages with bits and pieces of impressions and information. There is not a continual flow of one single impact. Raskin then concludes:

> Such information is internalized in us. The events go unexplained without a history and without an analysis. The world appears as discrete events and behaviors that are related through the presentation. But I become this unconnected puzzle piece. I understand things in undigested form without context. My public voyage is on a sea of unrelated behavior which screams at me to say that the society, and its method of communication, is dissociative.[3]

In somewhat the same vein Richard Adler argues:

> A book has a tangible physical existence. Films and plays begin and end in darkness and silence, which allows them to stand on their own. Television programs, by contrast, are surrounded by commercials and other programs. The English writer Raymond Williams has described this uninterrupted following of one thing by another as "flow," a characteristic which he believes to be central to the television experience, yet about which "it is very difficult to say anything." The reason for this difficulty, he explains, is that "it is a characteristic for which hardly any of our received modes of observation and description prepare us."[4]

Williams candidly acknowledges the problem of articulation that faces any media analyst. As stated, when faced with theater film and television, there are overwhelming similarities—thus the broad use of the term "film" in the volume. Yet there are also subtle but important differences which defy analysis except for those willing to dare highly tenuous theories. Given the design of this appendix, it would be futile to devise such theories, which would result in equally tenuous implications for the religious sense of reality.

To be specific about the uniqueness of television, one would have to go into the inner chambers of one's image flow. And such human dimensions have been very successful in defying controlled study or comment. Television's relation to human aggression is a case in point. Whether one uses clinical or correlational methods, combined with experimental in-laboratory or field settings, one faces mammoth methodological problems.[5] The human's interaction with the environment is too complex to reduce to simple forms of measurement. Such work faces innumerable pitfalls. The report by the Surgeon General's Scientific Advisory Committee on Television and Social Behavior is a case in point. One can look at a report done under the support of that committee and the New York State Department of Mental Hygiene and find a statement to the effect that in interpreting their data "the most plausible single causal hypothesis would appear to be that preferring violent television fare in the third grade leads to the building of aggressive habits."[6] But such a statement is weighed with qualifications, and the data is susceptible to other interpretations.

Such studies do have a value, of course, despite their limitations. They sensitize the public to dynamics present in television and cause it to pause and consider what is being encountered and its possible effects. And when one is dealing with such basic movements to one's life, that may be the most valuable service that can be rendered. In other words, one who is taught to pause and think is challenged to take charge of one's own life.

With this charge of accountability as a background, the conclusions about television will be limited to its role as a social phenomenon as opposed to a study of its ever fluctuating themes or its subtle techniques.

Television as a force in daily life is tremendous. One fourth of the average person's day is spent in its presence. On a given Sunday evening at nine, television sets are on in "slightly more than two-thirds of all homes in the country."[7] For a program just to remain on the air during prime time it must attract at least twenty million viewers, and to be a force in the economic projection of a network the numbers must be considerably more. Such figures are truly overwhelming, and the impact of television must be significant.

Gerbner and Gross attempt to address television as a social phenomenon through the familiar comparison with the automobile. They note that the "automobile that burst upon the dusty highways of the turn of the century was seen by most people as just a horseless carriage rather than as a prime mover of a new way of life."[8] In a similar way antibiotics would be considered as simply a way of helping the human combat disease more effectively rather than a breakthrough that would radically alter the complex of life forms on earth. Television, likewise, is not simply a way of bringing movies into homes. It is a force that is changing life styles in a persistent and relentless way.

Its growth has been phenomenal—from barely 100,000 sets in the United States in 1948 to fifty million in 1959.[9] In a little over two decades television has gone from an oddity in a few select homes to where its absence from a given household is a rarity. As a force in human life, therefore, it has challenged most other institutions as the prime molder of human values. It has at least challenged the family as the prime community. There are few families which have six hours of conversation in a given day. And even granted that communication involves much more than verbal exchange, one certainly must doubt how intense the exchange is on any level when compared to a child's absorbing involvement with the adventures of the latest superhero. Or one may take the millions of soap-opera viewers each afternoon across this country. To the extent that one shares feelings of hate, love, jealousy, and hope with the characters of these manipulative flows, one should at least question whether they have become one's prime community—in short, in what other situations and how frequently does one share these feelings?

Television also challenges the church and the school in their traditional roles as educators and as instruments of initiation into the community world view. As the quote from Gerbner and Gross in the introduction indicated, the stories that make "people perceive as real and normal and right" given options to human living are no longer primarily supplied by the above institutions. Television through sheer exposure is a powerful force in claiming what life in our cities is like; what human families are and should be; what are people's hates, loves, and fears; and, if the preceding chapters have any validity, what the nature of the human drama is all about.

Just as the car is not a horseless carriage, just as antibiotics are not just another way of treating human ills, television is not simply a means of showing movies. The car replaced the horse-drawn buggy and became the dominant force in the economy and the structure of the urban area. Antibiotics tilted the life struggle in favor of human life to the point where it has gone from a minority force to a majority presence on the earth and thus threatens to alter radically the composition of life forms. In a similar vein television challenges traditional socializing institutions to such an extent that one would question whether the kind and pace of human development is not seriously altered.

Notes

1. Marshall McLuhan, *Understanding Media* (New York: Signet Books, 1966), p. 22.

2. Ibid., p. 319.

3. Marcus G. Raskin, "The Dream Colony," *Television Today*, ed. R. L. Stavins (Washington: Communication Service Corporation, 1971), p. 16.

4. Richard Adler, "The Introduction: A Context for Criticism," *Television as a Cultural Force*, eds. Richard Adler and Douglas Cater (New York: Praeger Publishers, 1976), p. 7.

5. Seymour Feshback and Robert D. Singer, *Television and Aggression* (San Francisco: Jossey-Bass Inc., Publishers, 1971), p. 28.

6. Monroe M. Lefkowitz, et. al., "Television Violence and Child Aggression: A Followup Study," in *Television and Social Behavior*, eds. George A. Comstock and Eli A. Rubenstein (Washington: U. S. Government Printing Office), p. 84.

7. Adler, p. 6.

8. George Gerbner and Larry Gross, "Living with Television: The Violence Profile," *Journal of Communication* 25 (Spring 1976): 176.

9. Wilbur Scramm, Jack Lyle, and Edwin B. Parker, *Television in the Lives of Our Children* (Stanford: Stanford University Press, 1961), p. 1.

Bibliography

A. Religion and Film Books

The number of books in this area is indeed limited. Many listed here treat obvious moral questions on a popular level. As the preface indicated, there is not more than a handful of titles that treat the relationship in a serious academic manner.

Arnold, James W. *See Any Good Movies Lately.* Cincinnati: St. Anthony Press, 1972.

Cooper, John C., and Carl Skrade. *Celluloid and Symbols.* Philadelphia: Fortress Press, 1970.

Ferlita, Ernest, and John May. *Film Odyssey: The Art of Film as Search for Meaning.* New York: Paulist Press, 1976.

———. *The Parables of Lina Wertmuller.* New York: Paulist Press, 1977.

Getlein, Frank, and Harold C. Gardiner. *Movies, Morals and Art.* New York: Sheed and Ward, 1961.

Gibson, Arthur. *The Silence of God.* New York: Harper and Row, 1969.

Hurley, Neil P. *Theology Through Film.* New York: Harper and Row, 1970.

Kahle, Robert, and Robert E. A. Lee. *Popcorn and Parables.* Minneapolis, Minn.: Augsburg Publishing House, 1971.

Konzelman, Robert G. *Marquee Ministry.* New York: Harper and Row, 1972.

Lynch, William. *The Image Industries*. New York: Sheed and Ward, 1959.

Schillaci, Anthony. *Movies and Morals*. Notre Dame: Fides Publishers, 1968.

Schrader, Paul. *Transcendental Style in Film*. Berkeley: University of California Press, 1972.

Walls, James M. *Church and Cinema*. Grand Rapids, Mich.: William B. Eerdmans Publishing Company, 1971.

B. Selected Books

Many of the underlying questions confronting the serious study of religion and film are found in works probing the nature of religion and story, religion and the imagination, and religion and culture. The following is a selected list.

Arnheim, Rudolph. *Visual Thinking*. Berkeley: University of California Press, 1969.

Auden, W. H. *The Dyer's Hand*. New York: Random House, 1968.

Berger, Peter L. *The Precarious Vision*. New York: Doubleday and Company, 1961.

Burke, Kenneth. *Grammar of Motives*. New York: Prentice-Hall, 1945.

Campbell, Joseph. *The Hero with a Thousand Faces*. New York: Meridian Books, 1956.

Cox, Harvey. *Feast of Fools*. Cambridge: Harvard University Press, 1969.

Dunne, John S. *A Search for God in Time and Memory*. New York: Macmillan Company, 1969.

———. *Time and Myth*. Garden City, N.Y.: Doubleday and Company, 1973.

Esslin, Martin. *The Theatre of the Absurd*. Garden City, N.Y.: Anchor Books, 1961.

Funk, Robert W. *Language, Hermeneutic and Word of God*. New York: Harper and Row, 1966.

Frye, Northrop. *Anatomy of Criticism.* Princeton: Princeton University Press, 1957.

Gadamer, Hans-Georg. *Truth and Method.* Translated by Garret Barden. New York: Seabury Press, 1975.

Grotjahn, Martin. *Beyond Laughter.* New York: McGraw-Hill, 1962.

Hart, Ray L. *Unfinished Man and the Imagination.* New York: Herder and Herder, 1968.

Hauser, Arnold. *The Social History of Art.* New York: Knopf, 1951.

Hyers, M. Conrad, ed. *Holy Laughter.* New York: Seabury Press, 1969.

Langer, Susanne K. *Feeling and Form.* New York: Charles Scribner's Sons, 1953.

Lynch, William. *Christ and Apollo.* New York: Sheed and Ward, 1960.

————. *Christ and Prometheus.* Notre Dame: University of Notre Dame Press, 1970.

————. *Images of Faith.* Notre Dame: University of Notre Dame Press, 1973.

Martin, F. David. *Art and the Religious Experience.* Lewisburg: Bucknell University Press, 1972.

Niebuhr, H. Richard. *The Meaning of Revelation.* New York: The Macmillan Company, 1941.

O'Brien, William James. *Stories to the Dark.* New York: Paulist Press, 1977.

Richardson, Robert. *Literature and Film.* Bloomington, Ind.: Indiana University Press, 1969.

Scott, Nathan. *The Broken Center.* New Haven: Yale University Press, 1966.

————. *The New Orpheus.* New York: Sheed and Ward, 1964.

Te Selle, Sallie McFague. *Speaking in Parables.* Philadelphia: Fortress Press, 1975.

Van der Leeuw, Gerardus. *Sacred and Profane Beauty.* Nashville, Tenn.: Abingdon Press, 1963.

Vos, Nelvin. *The Drama of Comedy: Victim and Victor*. Richmond, Va.: John Knox Press, 1966.

Wiggins, James, ed. *Religion as Story*. New York: Harper and Row, 1975.

Wilder, Amos. *The New Voice*. New York: Herder and Herder, 1969.

Index

Adler, Richard, 166
Allport, Gordon, 25
American Graffiti, 53
Aristotle: on images, 5–6; on mimesis, 53
Armes, Roy, 136, 144
Arnheim, Rudolph: on film and expressionism, 142; on perception and culture, 61–62; on perception and simplicity, 60; on perception and thinking, 40
Art: and its peculiar language, 51; and religious consciousness, 50–51
Augustine, 6
Auteur theory, 145–47
Avant-garde theory, 147–51

Babbitt, Irving, 86
Balázs, Béla, 133, 140–41, 148, 151
Barth, Karl, 26
Bazin, André, 137
Being: in Aquinas, 48; in Heidegger, 48; in participative and religious experience, 47; as reflected on during cultural consolidation, 32; as a term for religious, 27; as a term rejected, 49–50; as used in religion and art studies, 47
Beings: as compared to Being, 47; as denied to theoretical reason, 49; and principle of relativity, 50; as studied by film, 48; as transformed by art, 47; as translated into Being, 52
Bells of St. Mary's, The, 68
Bergman, Ingmar, 99, 100
Biblical spectaculars, 66–67
Bregman, Lucy, 105–6

Brett, George Sidney, 5
Butler, Ivan, 146

Campbell, Joseph, 107
Candidate, The, 96–97
Cassirer, Ernst, 42
Casty, Alan, 130
Cavanagh, Ronald R., 23
Chauncy, Charles, 39
Clockwork Orange, A, 81
Colossus: The Forbin Project, 82–83
Come to the Stable, 68
Conceptualists and the origin of thought, 8
Cosmic photography, 54
Cox, Harvey: on fantasy, 105; on the secular, 94
Crites, Stephen, 115

Dekeukeleire, Charles, 132
Democritus, 5
Depth model: attraction for film maker, 104; potential for religious, 104
Descartes, René, 8
Devil films, 69–70
Dewey, John, 24
Direction in life, 59
Dixon, John W., 50–51
Dr. Strangelove, 81
Drama and movements of life, 61–62
Dreams: and images, 4; and myths, 107; and stories, 20

8½, 101–4
Elvira Madigan, 89–90
Epicureans, 4

Evans, Donald D., 25
Existence as term for religious, 27
Exorcist, The, 69
Expressionism in film, 140–52

Feast of Fools, 105
Fellini, Federico: and *8½*, 101; projecting fears, 62–64; on realism, 144
Film: affecting spirit through senses, 132; and audience, 130–34; and auteur theory, 145–47; compared to painting and sculpture, 41–45; compared to still photography, 45; and the dialogue between artist and world, 41; and expressionism, 140–52; extending human vision, 52, 54–55, 132; and framing effect, 54; and microscopic photography, 54–55; and montage view of, 44; presenting movement of life in complete forms, 53; producing total environment, 45–46; and realism, 134–40; and redemption of physical reality, 135–36; and religious dimension, 52, 55; and the role of sound, 44–45; and social identity in religion, 161–62; and spiritual identity, 156–59; and story, 114–15; and thematic identity in religion, 159–60
Film critics, the role of, 130
Frame effect, 54
Frankenstein Created Woman, 70–71
Funk, Robert W., 38

Gadamer, Hans-Georg, 119, 121–22
Gerbner, George and Larry Gross, 20, 168
Gessner, Robert, 131
Ghost and Mrs. Muir, The, 72
Giannetti, Louis, 136
Golden Notebook, The, 119
Gernall, Thomas: on God-world relationship, 63; on phantasms, 38–39
Gospel According to St. Matthew, The, 124
Greatest Story Ever Told, The, 67
Ground of Being: as term for religious, 27; as used in religion and art studies, 47; and a work of art, 51

Gulley, Norman, 5

Hart, Ray L., 38
Hart, W. S., 124
Heaven Can Wait, 71
Heidegger, Martin: on Being, 49; on images and words, 11; and role in religion and art theory, 47
Heraclitus, 4
Heroes: in human consciousness, 3; comparison of, 124
Hofstader, Albert, 42
Hurley, Neil P., 94

I Never Sang for My Father, 95–96
Images: as actions, 12; as archetypes, 107; and basic role in consciousness, 4–5; as bridge between perception and thought, 41; and continual tension of inner and outer origins, 9; dismissed as too static, 12; in dreams, 4; in early Christian thought, 6; in Greek thought, 4–6; as impression on the mind, 4; as medium for less significant thought, 10–11; in modern thought, 8–9; replaced by charts and diagrams, 10; and role in religious consciousness, 39–40; and synthesis of inner and outer history, 9; and words, 10–11
Imagination: and cultural confusion, 33–34; and the culturally accepted, 19; defying definition, 15; determining possibilities of religious thought, 29; equated with faith, 30; and experience, 30; in human consciousness, 16–17; in reference to relativity and subjectivity, 16; in religious consciousness, 22; and simplicity, 60
Imaginative constructs: produced by culture, 19; producing sense of direction, 59; role in human consciousness, 18
Imagists and the origin of thought, 8, 13
Intermediary theology, 53

James, William, 28
Jesus Christ Superstar, 68

Jung, Carl, *Memories, Dreams, Reflections*, 105

Kant, Immanuel, 49
Kanter, J. R., 8
Kaufman, Gordon, 40
Kelman, Ken, 148-49
Kinder, Marsha and Beverle Houston, 80, 81
King of Kings, 67
Klinger, Eric: on creativity and determinism, 9; on fantasy, 106
Kracauer, Siegfried, 135-36, 138
Kuhns, William and Robert Stanley, 46

Langer, Susanne, 41, 109
Lessing, Doris, 119
Lilies of the Field, 94-95
Lindgren, Ernest, 138
Lisieux, Thérèse of, 1
Lowe, Victor, 50
Lynch, William: on images underlying thought, 38; on imagination, 18; on faith and imagination, 30; on tenets of supernatural, 64

McLuhan, Marshall, 144, 165
Marrett, Robert R., 25
Martin, F. David, 46-47
Meaning as a human construction, 114
Mekas, Jonas, 150
Merton, Thomas, 1-2
Microscopic photography, 54
Mohammad, Messenger of God, 67
Movies: triviality of, 2

Narrative: as altering experience, 119; in initial experience, 115
Newhall, Beaumont, 42
Ninotchka, 132

O'Brien, William James, 122
Omen, The, 69
Otto, Rudolph, 24, 28

Painting, theories of, 41-42
Perception: categories of, 7; as interpretive, 8; and relation to thought, 40;

and simplicity, 60
Photography, theories of, 42
Planet of the Apes, 78
Plato, 5
Prayer and the use of art, 157
Presence as term for religious, 27
Process model: and biological mutations, 78-79; and cosmic development, 79-82; and culture 74-75; and mechanical mutation, 82-83; and religious potential, 76-77
Price, Henry H., 8, 12, 13
Pudovkin, V. I., 44, 143

Ramsey, Ian T., 17
Raskin, Marcus, 166
Realism in film, 135-40, 141
Realists and the origin of thought, 8
Reflection: and abstraction, 115; basic purpose of, 115; limits of, 114; and maintaining perspective, 113; necessity of, 113; and remembering, 115-16
Religious: and cultural confusion, 32; definition of, 23-29; as extraordinary sense of reality, 27; importance of, 113; working definition, 28-29
Remembering: altered by purpose, 14; as a basic form of reflection, 115
Reviews, purpose of, 122
Rhinoceros, 53
Richards, I. A., 54
Ricoeur, Paul, 33
Romantic model: basic tenents, 87-88; compared to eighteenth century, 84; compared to process view, 87; and counterculture, 85; and panentheism, 87; and reason, 86
Romeo and Juliet, 90
Rosellini, Roberto, 144

Sartre, Jean-Paul: position on images, 11-12; rejection of his position, 14
Schleiermacher, F. E. D., 24, 25
Secular model: compared to process, 90; and culture, 90-91; possible definitions, 92-93; and religious consciousness, 92

Seldes, Gilbert, 162
Shiner, Larry, 92–93
Singer, Jerome L., 21–22
Slow motion, 52
Smith, Huston, 114
Stoics, 4
Stories: and dreams, 21; in human consciousness, 20; in quest for human meaning, 115; in religious studies, 126
Stephenson, Ralph and Jean R. Debrix, 141, 143
Summer Wishes, Winter Dreams, 99
Supernatural model: and basic tenets, 64–65; and biblical spectaculars, 66–67; and comedies, 71–72; and devil pictures, 69–70; and traditional hierarchy, 64

Telescopic photography, 54
Television: as challenge to church and school, 169; and dream sequences, 166; and its growth, 168; and problem of articulation, 167; and violence, 167
Te Selle, Sallie McFague, 53

Thought as continuity and creativity, 14
Tillich, Paul, 25, 47
Time-lapse photography, 54
Tumbleweeds, 124
Two for the Road, 131
2001: A Space Odyssey, 79–82

Visconti, Luchino, 144

Wach, Joachim, 25
Walkabout, 88–89
Wall, James M., 67
Waltons, The, 53
Whitehead, Alfred N., 46, 50
Whittemore, Robert C., 39
Wiggins, James, 34
Wilder, Amos, 33–34
Wild Strawberries, 99, 99–101
Windelband, Wilhelm, 5
Wittgenstein, Ludwig, 10
Words, role in religious thinking, 38

Youngblood, Gene, 150

Zavattini, Cesare, 136–37